LOVE
&
LIGHT
From All There Is

Oceana and the Twenty-Four
Trance-channeled by

ZOETHA AMRITAM

BALBOA.PRESS
A DIVISION OF HAY HOUSE

Balboa Press books may be ordered through booksellers or by contacting:

Balboa Press
A Division of Hay House
1663 Liberty Drive
Bloomington, IN 47403
www.balboapress.com
844-682-1282

Print information available on the last page.

ISBN: 979-8-7652-4995-6 (sc)
ISBN: 979-8-7652-4997-0 (hc)
ISBN: 979-8-7652-4996-3 (e)

Library of Congress Control Number: 2024903991

Balboa Press rev. date: 03/21/2024

CONTENTS

CONTENTS

PREFACE

Love and Light from All There Is ... Love Is Beyond Existence

We have come here to share and honor you; to bring higher consciousness and love and light from all there is. The Divine is helping you people on Earth to raise your consciousness and open your hearts, raising your vibration with love with the help of us (Oceana and the Twenty-Four) and Amritam. That's why this book is a gift to the people of the Earth ... from the love of all there is. We are going to speak on love that is beyond existence. It is an honor for us, the Twenty-Four, to also do this book. It is not only important for your reality but also for our reality. As love is beyond existence, it's not only for your Earth but for other existences as the Earth rises. As love is beyond existence, it is understood and given and is rising on your Earth what will happen slowly; slowly, the world will rise in its vibration. The words "love is beyond existence" are so big that you can't imagine. That is the beauty of all this. We have come back to Earth to share, talk, teach, and speak to many people through the book, and maybe later in a crowd or maybe privately. As I start this book, I (Oceana) want each person to know in their world that love is beyond existence. Beyond that is the Absolute. Beyond the Absolute is beyond anything you can imagine. There's no name. We have come not only moving through Amritam, but there are many other beings of light that are in the room tonight wanting this book to start. So what is love? And what is love beyond existence? Love is actually the Absolute of all existence. Without love there is no existence. In all levels of awareness, consciousness, dimensions, planets, stars, galaxies, and other worlds, without love there would be no existence of any of it. So it's time to bring the energy of love to share with all of you the importance of love beyond existence. For, as your world begins to rise again in consciousness, awareness, and love beyond existence, it means this Earth is rising in a positive way. So it's time to give the information to the beings who live here. Many of the new beings and their parents are old, ancient souls and have signed up to help bring this Earth to a place of love beyond existence. This means there's so much immensity of awareness, consciousness, caring, learning, giving, transforming, and uplifting this planet and the people on it to the state of love beyond existence. Your planet has been working toward that for a very, very long time, along with other planets. It's time now to share that information with your Earth. It's time to bring people together with that knowledge. Many others do understand that and have known that there are seeded beings about love beyond existence on your Earth and on other planets as well. In the universe we (Oceana and the Twenty-Four) are in a state of rising into higher consciousness, higher awareness, higher beauty, higher compassion, and higher love. Many of the new children coming to your planet have immense states of love just in their very presence of being. As they grow and rise, they will be helping on this planet and bringing knowledge that has not been given yet. It wasn't ready, so that is why we are starting this book of love and light from all there is. Love is beyond existence. This book is for all human beings on this Earth. We have come from a long, long way to bring this knowledge to you, as well as many others who are coming to this planet to support it, to help you rise, and to give knowledge, higher intelligence, and eventually ancient, ancient, ancient secrets that will transform everyone on this planet to a state of unbelievable compassion and love. That is what this book is about. Love is beyond existence that you know, and we've come to share it with you on behalf of all there is. Just remember that. It's beyond anything you could ever imagine, but all of you can reach it. That's what everybody is longing for: to experience that existence when they have that moment of oneness. But it's beyond that. Nobody has gone there yet. They've experienced oneness through sexuality, meditation, drugs, dissolving into the wall, whatever, but they've never experienced ... love beyond existence!

INTRODUCTION I
About Oceana and the Twenty-Four

This is Oceana and the Twenty-Four. We, as a cluster of twenty-four enlightened beings in the Heavens, have always sent Divine Beings to come through or be channeled by human beings on the Earth and other planets. The Council of Beings that come to the Earth like me, Oceana, aim to help humanity raise their awareness. This planet is in a very high state of rising and slowly, slowly balancing the people who are on Earth to move into love, peace, and harmony. Although there is still a lot of work to happen here, it's beginning and the consciousness is rising. The Divine and the Absolute are giving knowledge through Amritam to help humanity and raise the vibration of your planet. As this book is written, it will uplift humanity. I'm here to transform this whole world along with many, many, many other entities and light beings.

The Twenty-Four are light beings that are powerful, and they are protecting your Earth. There are four to ten other groups in the universe that are protecting the Earth with love and light, and they are also sending other beings that are more conscious and aware to uplift your planet because not everybody is very uplifted yet. So we are working on sending more conscious leaders to keep this planet in a place of harmony with no wars. There are still lots of levels of lower consciousness on this planet, but it's slowly rising. Oceana is a group of twenty-four, and I'm the main speaker. I do speak to the others in the group if I have questions or ideas, and we still meet together on other dimensions, and it seems to be going very well. People love the work we do for them, and they are helped and they rise in consciousness. We all work together, all twenty-four of us, and we all help each person who comes for a private session on many levels. We help them mentally, physically, emotionally, and spiritually. If they are truly interested and we are the right ones for them, during a private session, we usually give a beautiful recorded meditation for them on a CD or give them a way to help raise their vibration and to move into forgiveness and love. All of us (the four to ten groups in the universe that are protecting the Earth) are working together to bring love, peace, harmony, joy, abundance, and balance to the planet. Not just to the planet, but to the people who are here. Those who are not ready to raise their consciousness and open up their hearts will be lifted up and given higher awareness so that they can help the Earth. There are only eternal upliftments, learning, growing, and transformation.

We are also called the Guardians. There are four groups of Guardians. We are one of them. Our group has twenty-four entities. There's one group that has fifteen entities, there is one that has twelve, and there is one that has eighteen. We are all here to help awaken you to the knowledge of your ancient soul that lies within you, and to help you bring love, peace, and harmony to your world. When you read this book, your heart and soul will open to who you really are, which is the spark of love that calls you home to your true self. It's time now to discover the ancient one that each of you are, that has come to bring healing, oneness, and joy to all beings on the Earth.

How Oceana Came through Amritam in the Beginning

This is Oceana and the Twenty-Four. We have been coming through Amritam since 1987. This is some of her background and how I came to her in the beginning. She had been studying meditation, consciousness, and awareness for a very long time with different masters and teachers. Amritam had been a very beautiful meditator and had been with different masters for a short time before she met Osho. She was very conscious and very aware, and her upliftment of consciousness was given to her by each master she studied with. She met and worked for a teacher named Werner Erhard. She studied with and helped set up workshops for Lazarus, a loving, wise, and ancient channeled being. She also studied meditation for a short time with an Indian master named Muktananda. After that, Amritam went to study meditation with Bhagwan Shree Rajneesh (Osho) at his ashram in Puna, India. We knew him (Osho). We knew his job. That's why Amritam had to go to him. She had no choice, really. She had to be there because she was part of the Council. Before she went to see Osho, she just thought she was looking for a teacher (she had been going from master to master at the time, and she didn't really know what she was doing). Amritam recognized Osho, and she knew she had to go there because she knew he was part of why she was on the Earth. She had to learn from him, and he gave her a lot of awareness and consciousness to go into the world with the Divine's message. As a result of being with Osho and later channeling us (Oceana), Amritam had no idea of what had been given to her job. It was good to not know, because she might have gotten scared or run away. We are talking about years ago when she first started channeling Oceana. Amritam was taught by Osho and many other teachers there, and she assisted in different groups, helped people a lot, and just was a being who knew what to do. She studied that for a very long time in Puna, India. They had teachers who taught Osho meditations, and encounter groups and awakening groups. She would assist all those groups, whichever one they gave her that day, and would learn and was taught how to lead the groups. She was taught, and that's how we knew she was strong enough to do it. Her love would carry her through to find the right places. She kept on advancing, and when Osho's Ranch ended, she came to Boulder, Colorado, and was doing rebirthing and massage and working with people like she had for Osho. We found out that Amritam would be a great person to move through from beings in the soul world who knew her well. They suggested her to us because she is very open, she has no blockages, she understands channeling, and she had raised her consciousness through Osho, other enlightened masters like Muktananda, and other ones she had met. Her vibration had been raised quite high. Since Amritam had a connection with channeling, the beings in the soul world who knew her suggested to us and the Council that she would be a good channel and that she would understand it and it wouldn't be hard for her to just close her eyes and leave her body so that we could come through to help humanity on a higher level of awareness. We brought dreams to her, telling her that we wanted to speak to her and come through her and help humanity. We asked her to get the people who were living in the house, and she started channeling to them, and then we came through. That is what happened, so she agreed to channel us when we appeared and talked to her and didn't frighten her or anything, because she understood it all. She started to channel, and we made agreements with her to protect her body, heart, and soul. When she is out of her body and channeling, there are other people who are very qualified to hold the space in the room. She agreed to channel, and we started doing lots of channeling for people in your world and helping them. So that's how it started, because she was such an open being that it's easy to move through her. When we first came through Amritam, the people there said I needed to pick a name, so we picked Oceana. "Ocean" because it is vast, "cean" is the wind, and "ana" is the female aspect of the Divine. So our name is Oceana. Amritam wanted us to have a name, but we didn't have names in the soul world, so that's the name we took. It was a perfect name. She liked it, and we liked it. Then she started channeling one-by-one, mostly for people whom she already knew from being with Osho. So that is how it all came about. It was quite beautiful, and we have agreements to always not hurt her body and to take care of everyone around her. We are very honored to come through Amritam because she is a pure being. She is love itself, and she also is very honest, real, and kind; and so, that kind of feels like how Oceana and the Twenty-Four are. Amritam can bring other enlightened ones through her too. Slowly, it has gotten bigger and bigger, but we haven't put any books out, and we are going to do that now because your world is ready now for help from different dimensions in the universe to help this Earth keep rising in consciousness, awareness, and love.

Now, thirty years later, it is another dimension where your planet is rising in consciousness, and people actually need more help because there is very powerful energy of this planet rising in consciousness and enlightenment. Slowly, slowly, all the beings of light with Oceana and other great, enlightened ones that are not in body are helping your planet rise, are helping people become more conscious, and are helping them to do meditations. There's been many masters sent here. Enlightened ones like the Rinpoches, Osho, and others. We will still be here to help humanity, and we are available to come and speak to people. All things are opened, and so we have spent many years speaking with and talking to people, especially the younger people. Channeling was very new at that time, although channeling has been on your Earth forever because that was the only way we could bring messages to the people on the Earth, so we would help those that would be born to have the ability in their brains to receive messages and channel and transform things. Amritam is one of those people; there are others, but not as many as there used to be long ago. Some people are what they call awakened conscious channels. They remember what they say, but Amritam has memories of a little bit before and sometimes later, but she does not remember what we talked about. That's a good thing because her being is holding the space, and her electrical systems work with the higher realms, and she has to hold that energy as well as the energy of putting out the information coming through her. A lot has happened since we began channeling, and there are many, many, many, many beautiful recordings that can be slowly revived later on, but not now. What we are doing now is putting out this book, *Love and Light from All There Is*, so we can tell people and bring them a story of humanity and what is going on out there. The background for this book should be a sense of celebration. We want this book to uplift people with love, caring, and joy. It will be an enlightened planet in the future. We want people to understand that they have the power to transform and change the directions. It takes awareness, consciousness, truthfulness, and honesty; it takes money; it takes the ability of people to begin to believe in meditation and God and all there is. It takes courage to step forward and speak the truth in every country, for in each country there is a group of people who are also aware of entities like Oceana and are being given information. Now things are quite different. We have to kind of start over. That's why this book is coming out. To let people know it's time to uplift, to transform, to change; and even the masters who are around will also read the book and get messages of what they are supposed to do. They don't know that yet. With Osho there was a lot for Amritam personally to learn. There was a lot for us to learn on Earth, such as how to speak with people and how to work with people, because we also had to come here and learn, too. So we learned from Amritam and people who were around her. We had to learn how to handle what Americans are like, and we got to see what Germans (and people from France, England, India, and different countries, for example) are like. It's taken us a long time. Your time is different than ours, but it seems through the years we had to learn a lot to help, and that's still going on. So this is the beginning of putting a book out about how the soul world has come to help all the souls that used to be in the soul world and have forgotten what their jobs were and what they need to do to bring love, peace, and harmony, and how to activate their highest consciousness, which is enlightenment. When that happens, everyone learns how to call forth and connect with their higher consciousness, which is light which every human being has. They will listen to the knowledge that the ancient ones are giving them, and they will change how they see the world. I'm talking about thousands of men and women who will remember they have come from a higher-consciousness state of love, forgiveness, abundance, happiness, purity, and caring for themselves—including all the countries and all the Earth—by trying to slowly bring knowledge to everyone with love. Part of the problem we are having on the Earth is that there are so many different directions going on, so many cultures and so many different ways people were brought up. They were trying to bring a sense of purity and love, but it's not easy; it's going to take time. It is better than it used to be, and it's slowly happening. Love is the keyword here. Respect and love; honoring each other; learning from each other; caring for your planet; caring for the universe; caring for the heart; and caring for balancing those who are imbalanced, and getting them healed, helped, uplifted, and restarted.

INTRODUCTION II

Amritam's Love Affair with the Divine (Written by Amritam)

My love affair with the Divine started as a young child. I was really longing to be with the Divine. I knew that I had come here on the Earth to be with God. I was really crying every day for God. Some days, I was just inconsolable ... crying for God. I would ask my mom and dad about where God was and where Jesus was, and I would tell them that I really wanted to go home because that's where my home was ... with God. My dad would try to console me and told me that God was in Heaven, and I would say that I needed to go back home. My dad said, "Your home is here now, with us, but you can always call His name and He will be near you." That got me to relax about it all. My mom and dad were very beautiful people. My dad was an entertainer, and we would travel everywhere. I just knew I was supposed to be with God, and so I was sort of looking to find the Divine again. As a child, I would see Jesus, or I would see Mary come to the foot of my bed, so I knew I would be protected and loved. One day, I was really upset and was missing God, and I ran away from home and went into a church and prayed to God and stayed there for a long time. While I was in the church, the Divine said to me, " Do not worry; just go home, and everything will be OK." I walked all the way back home and kept crying, but I really felt the Divine speaking to me. That was one of the bigger moments I had (the Divine speaking to me). I always felt really close to Mary and Jesus, and I had many, many questions about it. I had at least three or four visions of Mary and Jesus coming to the foot of my bed, because I would call for them; and if I was upset or if I was crying, they would come and tell me everything was going to be OK and they would take care of me. For me, that was kind of normal; it didn't seem special. I would call them, and they would come. As I got older, they didn't come like that anymore, but I always felt them there with me.

In my twenties I became interested in the new consciousness and awareness programs that were coming into the world, like EST (which was Werner Erhard, who was a big-time teacher then). He had big seminars and programs about consciousness, awareness, love, truth, honesty, and being real. That sort of consciousness started to come into the world, and I did those groups and I became very involved in that particular group with Werner Erhard. I ended up assisting when there were big groups with two hundred people. I learned a lot. I worked in the offices of EST, I assisted groups, and I would watch Werner Erhard teach. With these groups I met together with lots of people, and I became more conscious and aware. Then I started hearing about masters and teachers coming to America. There was kind of a flood of them coming to the Bay Area in California at that time.

Studying with Enlightened Masters

My love affair with the Divine led me to many teachers and masters who gave me upliftments of consciousness and awareness which prepared me for channeling Oceana later.

After working for Werner Erhard, I met Lazarus, who was a wonderful channeled being; and then I studied meditation with Muktananda, an enlightened master from India. All this prepared me to study with Osho in India. When I met Osho in person for the first time at his ashram in Puna, India, I took *sannyas* from him, and he gave me my name. He blessed me and touched my head and said my name was now Ma Prem Amritam. "Prem" means love, and "Amritam" means elixir, so my name means "love elixir." I passed out on the floor from his touch. He touched my head and he touched my third eye, and I passed out. The power of the energy of his touch went through my body, and I could barely walk. My soul was uplifted by being with him. Osho had a tremendous amount of energy that sent waves of love and power to you. When he would first walk into the hall, he would stand up and raise both hands and walk back and forth, sending blessings around the room to everyone. Many people would cry. Many people would feel this light coming toward them and would go into deep states of meditation. Sometimes, people were brought up to Osho to get a blessing from him. Each *satsang* was a little bit different. Sometimes, he would read to us or lecture to us. When he would talk, it was so unbelievably mesmerizing that I would go into deep states of meditation. It was like God was speaking to me. The way he spoke, the rhythm of his speaking, and the love that came through this man was huge, huge love. It was just waves of love going over the crowd, and everyone felt it. Everyone was blessed, and everyone was given an upliftment into their lives of awakening, consciousness, awareness, and forgiveness. I assisted in the meditation and therapy groups which helped transform people's lives. I became a therapist there. I just knew how to do it. It was there inside of me. When people release the pain and suffering from their lives, they are able to forgive and become empty. When you become empty, the Divine can flow through you. That's a very important point when I speak of my time with Osho. Being at Osho's ashram truly changed my whole life. I opened my heart to loving people, to loving myself, and to forgiving myself. It was an awakening for me on all kinds of levels! After being with Osho and receiving upliftments of consciousness and blessings from him, Oceana and the Twenty-Four came to me in dreams and asked to come through me to help humanity. In the dreams they would stand at my feet, and they were surrounded by beautiful golden light. They said, "We have come here to speak through you." I had never thought of myself as being a trance-channel before, so I thought I was just having amazing dreams, and I didn't think anything more about it. They would come in my dreams and say, "Just sit down and close your eyes, and we will come through." Then, one day, a friend of mine knocked at my door and told me she'd just had a dream that a light being told her to tell me that I was not listening to them, and all I needed to do was sit down and close my eyes and they would come through me! So, with my friend there, I sat down, closed my eyes, went inside, and was gone. Oceana came right through and spoke to my friend sitting there in the room! They spoke in pretty, broken English and had kind of an accent like they still do now, and that's how the channeling started. So I agreed to channel them, and my love affair with the Divine continued to grow beautifully. I am honored and grateful to channel Oceana and the Twenty-Four. At the time, I thought channeling Oceana was a gift. I didn't think of it as part of my life purpose. I was just in love with God. It just happened to me. It wasn't anything I tried to do. The gift of Oceana is brilliant, caring, and loving, and they really know people. They would come in and know about people's lives and would help them. Oceana started teaching classes and retreats and giving private sessions, and I started a nonprofit organization which is now called the Oceana Light Foundation. Other enlightened beings come through me also, and they all give beautiful gifts to people, including how to love oneself, how to go into the Divine, and how to feel one's own ancientness and the light that each person carries and has forgotten. Oceana gives information of the Divine, God, where we came from, what we are supposed to do on the planet, and how to help each other. Oceana brings people back to the heart, their ancientness, and their love affair with God—and people are really touched by that. Oceana gives a lot of talks on forgiveness, awareness, and consciousness. We have many CDs on those topics. I can share my perspective on Oceana and other beings that have come through me. When Oceana comes through me, I feel this immense love, protection, kindness, and peace in my body. They are a very gentle energy; very loving, very warm, and very open to people who are speaking to them and asking help in meditation or in their lives or in understanding what the Divine is and what God is. Oceana would speak to people of those things, and their hearts would open. My heart opens when I bring Oceana through. I noticed I was very much softer, more gentle, and very loved by Oceana. They carry a huge amount of love and compassion for humanity, for people's problems, and for people who are looking to raise their consciousness and their love affair with God. They do a really good job of that. People are very touched; they are very loved and feel very cared for by Oceana.

When I channel and leave my body, this is what happens. I get the feeling that I am going to channel to people or that it's time to give information. I just close my eyes and go inside, and I ask the Divine to protect me. I ask Oceana (or somebody else, like Osho or anybody else that I channel) that they come. Then I say, "Dear soul, mind and body of the Divine, please protect me. Let only the truth and light come through me, and let only enlightened masters come through me. I only allow that." I close my eyes and I ask that they give only positive information and what people need. I also ask that they don't hurt my body in any way. I ask them to protect me and that only an enlightened being can come through me, and they protect my body so that I don't get sick. They made an agreement about that with me. I ask all that when I'm closing my eyes and letting them come through. Once I do that, it's sort of like my being just moves over, and then they come through and I'm held in light and in a beautiful state of meditation. When the Divine asked me to close my eyes long ago and open my heart, they said a being would move through me that would help many people in awareness, consciousness, and love of the Divine. When they came through, I remember feeling the Divine was using me as a vehicle to speak to humanity and to bring awareness, consciousness, healing, and love while giving these messages of the Divine to humanity. I was in deep gratitude and love about this because it helped me to awaken, to love and care for humanity in a most beautiful way as I experienced oneness ... one with all things.

Part of my job on Earth is to introduce masters to my meditation students in a spirit of oneness and service to the Divine, which I have done many times through the years. My love affair with the Divine led me to invite Master Sha to Boulder, Colorado, in 2008. He uplifts people's soul journeys on many levels and awakens them to the powers of the soul. I arranged a big workshop for Master Sha in Boulder where he suddenly downloaded many saints and healing angels into Baba's barn at the center that I ran on my property. I was truly honored, and the barn was transformed into a divine temple, which had been a lifelong dream of mine. I took care of it for years, and I really loved it dearly. Words cannot express the incredible honor and opportunity it was to serve the Divine in that way! I want to say to the people who read this book that my whole life changed with a whole new beginning because I met and channeled enlightened masters, and they blessed me and helped me. I am so grateful to them. These masters have the power of the Divine flowing through them to open up human beings who are on the spiritual path and need their third eyes opened. They need their chakras opened. They need their hearts opened. They need their brains to open. These masters are sent with the power to do that. The Divine flows through them and opens up people to their hearts, to love, to peace, and to understanding.

CHAPTER 1

The Magical Place

If you awaken, this is where you can go: the enlightened planet, Earth. As each of you read this book, you will slowly, slowly remember why you've come here and what you'll need to be doing to help raise your consciousness and your awareness. Also, as this occurs on your planet, there will be more and more divine, enlightened ones sent here to help all the different cultures. There are so many different cultures in Europe and in different countries, in Japan and China and Australia. There are people in so many cultures, and they all have different ways they have grown up. As a whole world of light, your planet is rising, and it will take some time. This is why we are writing the book: so you can be more patient and understanding of the planet you were born to and how difficult it is to create an enlightened planet, especially when you have all levels of consciousness. So, as you slowly become more intelligent, the divine sends more and more awakened ones; and as you are given more and more knowledge and support from the divine, all of this will slowly change. You've seen three hundred years ago what kind of state your planet was in. There has been knowledge given that has brought you to more awareness: cars, schools, teachers, equipment, computers, and technology. All of these kinds of things have made your lives easier, and along with that, you'll all rise in more and more awareness. Many of you will come back to the Earth numerous times. The Earth is not going to be completely enlightened for some time, but it is on its way, and that is why this book is being written. That is why you have enlightened masters on your planet. That is why you have the Karmapa and had Buddha, and you have had masters like Osho. There are other enlightened ones on your planet, like Master Sha, Braco, and a few more, especially in the Buddhist tradition. You have the Rinpoches, and you have the Karmapa—you have many. So you can see that, if you have this book in your hand, you are ready to become more aware, more conscious, and more enlightened and are looking to have a more peaceful and loving life. Maybe you are married, maybe you have children, maybe you are wanting those things. Maybe you are wanting to create a very highly awakened lifestyle by studying with these beautiful masters so that, when you have children, when you bring children in, you'll be bringing in more awakened children to a planet that is awakening and growing.

This planet is very beautiful, and it still has tremendous problems. Slowly, in time and with love, meditation, and more and more awakened souls, the planet will become a very peaceful place. There will be no more wars. There will not be so many "I'm better than you are" people. This will take time; and in time, people who are sent here will bring oneness everywhere. You'll have higher-consciousness people living here. This is not all going to happen at once, but it is what your world is planned for. So I have come, and other masters have come, to give you this book to see that things can change. Things can get more aware. Knowledge can be given, awakenings can occur, and caring can be spread all through your countries. People will help love each other and care for each other. This will take time. This will happen not only on this planet but also on other planets in your universe. Everything is rising into light. It is not happening in one day, but it is definitely occurring.

So this is kind of the story that we wanted to give to people with this book, to help them start thinking bigger and be more awakened. Look into meditation, find teachers, and find enlightened ones you are able to connect to, so that your soul is able to rise and become more conscious, more aware, and maybe more enlightened. This depends on you, your love, and your commitment to love, peace, harmony, upliftment, joy, and service to all those on the planet. As that happens, there will be more intelligent people who are uplifted who will come to the planet and will develop many new things to bring the world closer together. Phones did that, computers are doing that, and Morse code did that. So, slowly, we will be sending people who have intelligence that can bring the worlds together and bring communication together. More and more balanced people who are loved and cared for and are mentally well will come to this planet. Those who are moving through good/bad and right/wrong imbalances are slowly being uplifted right now on your planet. You will be seeing other planets also rising and coming to upliftment in your universe. There will be more and more enlightened teachers—like the Buddha, Jesus, and those who have come through the Buddhist tradition (like the Rinpoches and others)—so there will be all kinds of ways to rise to bring people to higher consciousness and enlightenment. This is where your world is coming to, and it's important to teach people meditation. It's important to write books to tell them that they have come here to uplift; to become more conscious; to be more caring; to learn to communicate with love, beauty, and joy; and to raise their children in love, beauty, and joy.

Slowly, there will be more very mentally balanced people who are of very high consciousness. For it is time for this planet to start rising more and more into enlightenment, into abundance, into beauty, into caring, into service, and into creating beautiful schools and beautiful colleges. It's not just like it is now. It's learning socializing with respect, love, and honoring each other. When you bring children into the world, the children are loved and raised with beautiful, caring enlightenment. Those who are ready to awaken and be in a state of love, caring, and joy will be coming to this planet because this planet will eventually be a very awakened planet. That is the goal here. That is why I'm here. That's why you've had all the masters you've had here. Buddha was one of them. There are very, very many Buddhas on your planet at this time. I won't name their names, but there are quite a few who are keeping your planet in harmony and also teaching you, giving you the experience of love, healing, understanding, and really deep caring. All the other ways of doing things for love are slowly being dissolved from this planet. So that's why we have come to move through Amritam, who is our only channel. We have many different beings here, and we have many teachers here. We have Master Sha, who is an enlightened one. There are many through the Buddhist tradition and other traditions of enlightened ones who are holding the space in that area. So, for those who are reading this book, I'm so delighted that you have found me, Oceana, and others who will be giving talks and workshops. You'll be invited to understand your place in this story of awakening this planet. Many of you are just waiting to be called and have been longing to find the ways to give your knowledge, give your love, and give your training for children and young people. I want this book to go into the deep soul of the people, for there are many things changing on your Earth. There are many shifts and changes in awareness and consciousness, and there have been enlightened ones given. Your world's going to change, and out of that change there will be a great celebration of love. There will also be a great sadness of the old that will leave. In this process it will transform like this. It won't be like this way is good and that way is bad. This is transformation, dancing together. We will look at how this worked and that worked, and how this didn't work and that didn't work, and how we're attached to life being this way and to life being that way. People will see that they will have to move to the now. Just like Osho said, you have to live here now. You cannot live in the history of your family. You can learn from the history of your family. You can learn from the mistakes of the governments. You can learn from the different cultures. You can learn from the British, the Germans, the Dutch, the Chinese, the Japanese, the Asians, and all the people. You must sit back and learn, love, and forgive. The biggest thing that has to happen on your Earth is forgiveness.

CHAPTER 2

The Calling

One of the things we are doing in this chapter is to call those souls who are ready to receive the important information we are here to give. We are calling you. We are calling those who have been given information, who have been given upliftments, and who have been given transmissions and knowledge to bring to the Earth. So we are calling you all, my dear ones.

We are calling your souls to let you know it is now time. Oceana and the Twenty-Four are calling you: the beloved ones of God's gifts, the ones who have been sent here. We are calling you home to bring the love, the consciousness, the beauty, the knowledge, and the immense understanding that all things come from the absolute, which is love. We have sent many special people (or beings or souls) to your planet to help humanity at this time. Slowly, slowly, dear ones, things will begin to transform. It will not happen all in one night. Transformation of this magnitude takes time. It will take time to erase the sadness, the pain, the hurt, the loss, the grief, the diseases, and especially the imbalances in the minds and brains of human beings. Through time, through meditations, and through the energy coming from the Divine

Ones in all the universes blessing your Earth to come home to its Source, transformation can occur. Through the purity, light, joy, caring, forgiveness, abundance, kindness, wealth, and the most beautiful moments of joy, the most beautiful beings of light will be born to your planet. The most beautiful moments of intelligence, knowledge, peace, and harmony are coming. These moments will bring this Earth into a state of such unbelievably high peace, love, joy, harmony, abundance, and happiness. We are so delighted as Oceana to be given by the Absolute this job to remind you who are seeded with this knowledge. We are calling you. As we are sharing, and as each of you read this book, you will be touched by the Absolute. It is time now, dear ones. It is time. Everyone who is reading this book or listening, just close your eyes and hold this book to your heart. Take a deep breath and relax. Say three times, "Beloved Absolute, I love you. Beloved Absolute, I love you. Beloved Absolute, I love you. Please awaken my knowledge within me to remember that I have come to the Earth to help humanity through love, joy, kindness, happiness, and abundance." Take another deep breath, relax, and know that as you read this book you are being called home. Not home like the house you live in or your home on another planet, but home inside yourself. Your soul is where you are at. This home, your soul, will be given so much knowledge, so much love, so much abundance, and so much happiness. This book will raise each of you in all countries to the place that you are to be taken to. It will not happen overnight, but in time. We are sending all our love; all our powers of peace, love, and harmony. We are sending intelligence, music, art, poetry, dance, meditation, awareness, and higher consciousness to bring this Earth into pure balance. To bring those who are ready into pure balance and to teach ones who need new knowledge. There will be blessings that will be given on your Earth to help people who have been in lower states of consciousness. They will be given blessings that will raise them into higher consciousness. Babies, children, all the people ... eventually, everybody will not be starving or in pain or having horrible diseases. Slowly, slowly, all that will be transformed on the Earth. Many enlightened beings from the other planets of higher love and awareness are coming to help you. We are all so delighted. We are all so grateful for this job. We are so happy to help awaken everyone to your higher consciousness of abundance, of love, of peace and harmony. Slowly, slowly, this will happen. It won't happen in one day. It will take years, but it will happen. Each of you will rise. I just want all of you who are reading this book to know that you are loved, you are abundant, and you will be given help to transform your personal lives, your health and relationships, your finances, and your children's lives. As you continue to read this book, feel the love of all the Divine Beings and saints in the heavens sending you love, blessings, peace, joy, happiness, a sense of higher intelligence, a sense of caring, forgiveness, and compassion. Feel a sense of relaxation and a sense of opening your third eye's vision so you can see the beauty in this world and in other worlds. People will have dreams, beautiful dreams and visions and messages given to them, and angels coming to them. It is all going to happen, dear ones. We, Oceana, are also receiving information and guidance from the Absolute because this world needs a tremendous amount of love and blessings given to it. The Absolute has called all the ancient ones from many, many, many centuries to come and help with the Earth. I know in the early days, when we first started channeling, we told you in the same kind of way that we've come to help, and we did balance things tremendously. It's now time to do that again, along with the help of many other amazing and powerful beings, awakened and enlightened ones, beyond enlightened ones, ancient ones, saints, angels, and Buddhas. They are all helping with the book and helping humanity.

They are helping with educating people about the Earth, about meditation, about who they are, about their souls, about their consciousness, about their awareness, and about their love. It's all been forgotten again; even though there have been many books written, we will write them again. So this is the beginning of our time to help humanity through books. In this timing there will be gatherings where people will come together to dance, move their bodies, and meditate. We will also develop some meditations that include movement as well as seated practices. These are all in the plans. Somewhere in your heart you have to speak to God. You have to look at your importance of why you are here on the Earth and what you are doing on the Earth. Have you really come to do the job you've been asked to do to help humanity? This is not a small story. There will be many, many other beings that will be involved. Some people are on the Earth to relearn compassion and love and to open their hearts more. Different planets have different jobs. This planet Earth is a planet of upliftments for people to come back and open up their hearts, consciousness, and awareness. So that's why we're calling you through love, consciousness, and awareness. There are many different dimensions on this planet. Through this book, people will be called to their assignments. Many people forgot their assignments because, when you come onto the Earth, you do forget your past and what your job is. You know as a child, and you're learning so much from what the Earth is anyway, but people forget that they have a calling. So we are going to remind you and try to gather you again through this book. When you read it, you will remember and you will contact us. People will be drawn that way. The right ones who are supposed to come will come. We are calling you! It is all going to happen, dear ones. We love you; we send joy, happiness, and love from Oceana and the Twenty-Four. Thank you, dear ones. We love you!

Meditation/Visualization: The Calling

Remember, you are the watcher; you are ancient, and you've come to this Earth to grow and to transform. Some of you have knowledge to help the Earth. Some of you have hidden gifts that will be given to the Earth in time. Some of you will help humanity and will help the Earth to stay safe with its rivers, with its mountains, and with its oceans. It's a very, very important time, dear ones. It's time to call you. I am Oceana ... I am the ocean. I am the wind, and I am the female aspect of the Divine. I have come to bring love to humanity. I am calling you, calling you along with great enlightened ones like Buddha and ancient masters. We are calling you, calling the young ones who have forgotten that they are the old ones. You are seeded with knowledge to help humanity. You have information in your cells. You have new ideas to help heal the Earth and to help people who have forgotten that they are all one consciousness on this Earth. All the different generations of light are coming to help your world; all the different countries in Europe, in Asia, all of you. All people, I am calling you. I am calling you to remember you are seeded ... those of you who are ... with knowledge to bring peace to your Earth; to bring awakening to your Earth; to bring love to your Earth; to bring peace to your oceans, peace to the mountains, rivers, and trees. People in the Himalayas and from all over the world are being called to go into meditation, to go into the light, to go into love, and to go into joy. All of you are being called. All of you are being asked to come to the light, come to oneness, and come to your world. Each of you who begin to meditate in your countries, in your small towns, in the mountains, by the oceans, all of you carry power when you meditate. Maybe when there is a storm coming and you all meditate together, you bring a hum and the storm quiets itself. Bring the hum of the Divine. When the

Divine hums, the world goes back into balance. Your world is shaky right now because there are so many different things going on. We are calling you to go into meditation. We are calling you to dance; we are calling you to call the ancient one with knowledge that's within you to bring awareness to this Earth, to bring peace to this Earth, bring joy to this Earth; and slowly, slowly, it will catch on. The dancing, the singing, will start coming if you all come together, if you all move to forgiveness, if you all open your hearts and souls. I am Oceana. I carry the ocean, the wind, and the Divine. Everyone carries the ocean in their hearts, the wind and the Divine. All of you, every single human being, were given seeds of the Divine ... whether you know it, whether you use it, whether you experience it is another question. Now, because there is so much shaking on your Earth, you must all come together in meditation, in peace, and in love to help humanity. I am calling you, Divine ones; I am calling you to come together with love and forgiveness. I am calling the ancient ones to remind you. I am calling your souls to awaken you with love, knowledge, and the dance of love for humanity and loving each other, supporting each other, taking care of the children, taking care of the schools, taking care of the land and the animals. Open your hearts, Divine Beings, on your Earth to awaken now. I am calling you; God is calling you; Oceana is calling you; enlightened masters are calling you to come together with love, light, harmony, balance, and meditation. We will slowly gather everyone and teach you meditation, teach you dance, teach you love, and teach you happiness. We love you and we honor you. Close your eyes and ask inside, "Dear soul of mine, give me my inner name. Give me my inner name." The soul in you, the soul in you, your inner name, the soul within you ... your inner name, your inner name ... the soul in you ... breathe. It's not hard; it's simple ... your inner soul. We'll help you become healthy, balanced, cured, open, and honest. Remember the ancient being meditator that you were; the monk that you were is here on this Earth, disguised to bring love, peace, and harmony together. The young people must awaken. They have a job, a big one, so I'm calling you. So, everybody, take a deep breath and thank your souls for coming. Thank your brains that got you here. Thank your hearts, thank your ancient souls inside, thank yourselves for loving yourselves and for forgiving yourselves any time you've hurt anybody or they've hurt you. Just know your soul is always with you. Always go into meditation when you need help, and ask for advice. Keep coming, dear ones. This is Oceana. "Ocean," "cean" is the wind, "ana" is the female aspect of the light. We love you. I send blessings to each of you. Love you, love you, love you ... here's the bell.

CHAPTER 3

Meditation

So this is Oceana, and we are going to do this chapter on meditation. Meditation is very, very, very important for all spiritual seekers and spiritual people. From the very beginning, there's always been a special prayer, or sitting and watching. This is very important for people to train their minds, to allow them to go inside to their souls and balance mental, physical, emotional, and spiritual bodies … mind bodies and soul bodies. The mind body is for keeping the body to work. The soul body is also responsible for that, but not in the same way. It's responsible for the soul that's within you. You have been given a chance to come to the Earth (or whatever planet you're on) so you can raise your consciousness, your awareness, and your intelligence. You've also been given the ability to move into a space of sainthood as well as the Divine. All of you carry the seeds of the Divine, and all of you carry the seeds of sainthood life after life. As you develop and become more conscious, more aware, and more intelligent in each life, you uplift if you come to the Earth or if you want to go to other planets. This is so beautiful because you get a chance every life to be more aware, more conscious, more loving, more intelligent, and more awakened, and you get a chance to experience more beauty. You will become a channel of light, a channel of love, a channel of being and caring and healing. All these things happen as you raise your consciousness life after life. One of the ways for that to happen is meditation, which can happen in all kinds of different ways. Some people need to move when they are meditating. Some people need to sit quietly. Everybody has to slowly train their minds to get quiet and slowly, slowly go in and be the watcher of the mind. As they practice meditation, I suggest for most people that they do movement first. That is what many masters have seen. Brand-new people cannot just instantly sit and meditate. It takes some time. It takes for you to relax. It takes for you to understand what meditation is. It takes for you to know you have a watcher. So you watch the mind, and slowly relax and go into deep states of meditation for many years and years, thousands of years. There's always been meditation of some sort given to higher-conscious people, and this has helped them to advance their brains and to advance their souls. When you meditate, the soul relaxes and it gives you the healing, love, and information that you need as a human being to advance your consciousness and awareness. As far as we're concerned, meditation is number one. It's what all people should be doing. Number one is meditating. It takes some time, though, because you have a busy mind. That's why you go to different masters and teachers; and even in the early days of church, that was what prayer was. It was meditation. When you call forth the higher awareness in you so that you can become more intelligent, more aware, and more balanced, even your body heals from meditation. You use more of that part of the brain that goes into higher levels of awareness, of beauty, of consciousness, and of the Divine. So you can see that meditation is really the biggie and the most important thing that all spiritual people need to do. Over the years, there's always been given different kinds of meditation, but what we think is when people first start to meditate and it's new for them, we like people to move, we like people to dance or shake or run or just move for a while. We loved Osho. He came up with many ways to meditate. He was one of Amritam's teachers. He was very successful with his movement meditations—dynamic, Kundalini, *nataraj*—all of those three were very powerful. So what happened when there was a lot of movement? People found that they could go easily into meditation and be relaxed and not be frustrated about meditating or expecting anything. Their bodies were already relaxed before moving and doing different movements. They would settle and go inside to their souls, to the being, to the presence of light within every human being. All human beings are at levels of consciousness, awareness, and meditation, but when you read this book, you will find what works for you. Amritam and I are giving some new meditations for people to do when they get the book. Meditation is where you connect with your soul and with the Divine. That is why so many people find their lives really work better when they meditate, because the silence is there. There isn't a lot of rushing around. Your world is very fast in rushing and coming and going. People really need to sit and connect with the soul, with the heart, and with God. It's very needed for your country, and actually, it's needed for every country. When people go into these states, they are balanced, and they can rise and experience light and enlightenment. Meditation is one of the main things that people do to awaken, and it's very important. Some people, especially in the beginning, need to do movement, and some people need to walk. They each will find when they go to a master or teacher which meditation clicks with them. When you know that, you go quickly and then you go into meditation much easier. You will have a more conscious awareness of your soul, of who you are, of what you do and don't do that's appropriate. You are able to examine yourself in a very beautiful way to uplift your consciousness, your love, your awareness, and the joy of being alive; the ability to sit with nature and the mountains, trees, sun, sunset, and the moon rising. You're able to let go, and your own soul will feel the love of the world, the nature, the birds, the oceans coming in and out, and streams coming from the mountains. There is so much beauty in your Earth, and when you meditate and go inside, you call forth the higher self of yourself, meaning your soul. You're able to rise through meditation and awaken your soul; more and more each life, you are able to awaken. Through meditation you can look inside and understand who you are and understand the Divine, understand God, understand the presence of your light in what level of awareness and consciousness you're at. So, when you go to an enlightened master, they help you rise. They help you become more awakened. Your brain expands and your soul is awakened inside. It's like you've been sleeping, and now you can awaken. We really love it when people sit and take time each life to honor their spiritual lives as well. You will see that different countries have been studying meditation for a very long time, and we—the Divine—have always sent enlightened ones to help humanity raise their consciousness, to become more aware and full of light. It has always been given, and if you look into the histories you'll see there were many monks and masters and ancient ones that came, like Jesus and Moses, and right now you have the Dalai Lama. You have a lot of different masters. Muktananda has left his body, and there are many enlightened ones up in the Himalayas whom nobody will ever know. Actually, those beings meditate a lot, and they actually keep the Earth more balanced. Many people don't know there are many, many people in the mountains of different countries who are meditating and helping hold this Earth in a peaceful place. My suggestion is that each leader in any country must have meditation in their heart. They must be a meditator who is getting messages from the Absolute and the inner soul. That's what is missing on your planet. You have to remember that this is about love, about consciousness, about service, about helping each other, about raising the awareness of each person with love and caring. Your Earth has had such a hard time with that. There are so many people who are homeless and are unable to eat, unable to care and understand or have the ability to learn and grow and connect with their souls. That's why this planet is not an enlightened planet. Because of that, we (not me, Oceana, but other enlightened ones) had set it up to have a planet to help everyone awaken to love, consciousness, and awareness. Many people are working out their negative karma through growing and through really opening up their hearts and meditating and wanting to help humanity. That was just because they didn't know about meditation and weren't taught. There are people on your Earth who have had times when there was so much karma and so many mistakes in their brains that it was just sad. Your country, your Earth, is a place of working out karma. Good karma and bad karma. Slowly, slowly, people are learning to love again, to have consciousness. And because you have so many people with negative mistakes in their brains and there are so many with pure minds (enlightened ones), it's a very difficult Earth. We're trying to bring it to a place of an enlightened Earth, which is not happening yet. Mother Earth will one day be an enlightened planet, and everyone will have their consciousness uplifted and will be raised to awareness, consciousness, and love. We are working on the creation of that plan so it can happen much faster. Now you're seeing lots of books being written and teachers coming forth. You've got lots of dualities happening here. Some are warring countries here, some are pure countries, and that is what the Earth is all about. We're trying as a whole—all the Absolutes—to bring the Earth up in consciousness. That will eventually happen. This book is being written to start the ball running or get it going so people begin to love again, open their hearts, forgive themselves, and forgive each other. How you dissolve all of the negative and positive things you've done is by practicing forgiveness. Forgiveness, forgiveness, forgiveness, forgiveness is number one for this planet. Forgive them; they know not what they are doing. That is what Jesus said on the Cross. Yes, forgive them. He forgave everyone. That's exactly what has to happen on your Earth. Forgive them; they know not what they are doing. They don't understand that their consciousness has not risen enough. We are sending love, sending great beings to your Earth, to help this world to eventually be an enlightened Earth. This is the beginning of it. Those of you who love; those of you who are balanced; those of you who are working to become mentally, physically, emotionally, and spiritually balanced ... your answer to help you do that is to forgive yourself and others. So that is what the Absolute is bringing to your Earth. Sending you great ones to help you do that through meditation, through love, and through understanding. People who have mental problems and things like that will eventually be healed and balanced mentally, physically, emotionally, and spiritually. At that time, this Earth will be full of light, and levels of consciousness will be raised to high states of purity and love, joy and happiness. This is why you are seeing different masters coming here. We are going to need more to help your Earth; and how you can help yourself, number one, is to find a teacher with whom you feel balanced, someone you feel connected with in your heart. This teacher will help teach you meditation and forgiveness. The only way out of your story is forgiveness, and that takes time. Some people have been hurt so deeply that it takes time for them to forgive.

Meditation will help you, and understanding humanity will help you. All those things will help you to purify yourself and have forgiveness for those who've hurt you. Forgiveness for yourself and to forgive yourself for the mistakes you've made, that's what we see here on your Earth. That's what we're working toward. That's why there are meditations in this book. That's why you have so many new enlightened masters, like Master Sha. There are other new and older masters who are still alive and are helping so many people to forgive, to awaken, and to raise their vibration. When you are in a state of loving yourself, loving others, and giving forgiveness, the Divine will rush to you and help you; slowly, slowly in time, when it's right to awaken you. If you meditate, if you are OK with sitting in the power of yourself rather than being run by your fears and worries, you will do much better. You have to trust the Divine and the God within you to support you. Ask God and the Divine to help you with this work to balance you mentally, physically, emotionally, and spiritually to help humanity, to help the spiritual presence of who you are, the god self of who you are. Move from that direction. You will be relaxed. Things will happen gently. You won't be in fear, and you'll have a good time. So think about what I'm saying. If you are in fear, you will create fear around everything. So I am here to bring light, love, abundance, joy, peace, and balance to people. That will happen for you, for this is not a small thing that I'm going to do. This book will help humanity because your world is having difficulty now. We will send huge amounts of love with armies of light beings. Armies ... and nobody will see them. I will give meditations; and when people do the meditations, they will do it from the God part of their hearts for humanity. It has to come from God, from humanity, from service, and it brings your world back to peace because it can happen now.

Oneness

For those who have been reading about meditation, one thing that happens out of meditation is that you realize you are one with everything. You even have direct experiences of that through your master and through your meditation, through understanding and through awareness. When people rise in consciousness and meditate, they go inside and they open their hearts. Most often, you have a direct experience that you are everything. That's an enlightened experience. When people have that enlightened experience, their brain cells change. All the separated brain cells that think that way are sort of not used anymore, so they disappear slowly. When the meditation is so strong, you have direct experiences that you are one with the birds, you are one with the sky, you are one with the ocean, you are one with the sun, you are one with the Earth under your feet, you are one with the smells of life, the beauties, the magic of human beings who are uplifted who are kind, joyous, celebrating, caring, and awakened. This is a very powerful upliftment planet that will be like that. When that happens, you have direct experiences of oneness and you are one with all of everything. How that happens is through meditation and coming back and forth to the Earth or another planet. This uplifts your soul so that you actually rise in intelligence and in meditation. You awaken and become enlightened. When you become enlightened there are different stages of enlightenment, so you start having experiences of oneness. When that happens, you have no anger in you. You are in love. You are one with the tree, one with the bird, one with the fly, one with the wind, the streams, and the clouds. You are one with the children and every person. You see your planet slowly rise, and everyone is in one consciousness of love. It's beautiful. It's serene. It is peace. It is welcoming; it is as if you experience God within you, the love within you, and the oneness of each person. They have arisen in awakening, in enlightenment, in beauty, and they have forgiven themselves; and in all other times in the early stages of developing, they have forgiven, forgiven, and forgiven. This is slowly what is happening on your Earth. Slowly, slowly, there will be people living in oneness here, there will be intelligence that is in oneness, that has a direct experience of oneness. That would be an enlightened planet. Your planet is not enlightened, but it has beings that are enlightened on it, and they are helping raise the consciousness. They are helping uplift your Earth with love, caring, and balance. Through time, through meditations, and through the energy coming from the Divine Ones in all the universes blessing you and your Earth to come home to its Source, transformation can occur. Their brains, their minds, their hearts ... everything is enlightened. This takes time. That's why, in each incarnation, you have to forgive, because there have been times when you weren't developed enough yet, when you made mistakes or you weren't taught or you weren't loved or cared for. So you're in a process of upliftment to the Absolute. It's where you've come from ... the Absolute. Every person is in a process of upliftment. It takes time.

After the Experience of Oneness

When you have raised your consciousness, you've had some experiences of being one with the trees, the moon, the stars, the Earth, with your beloved, with the children, with everything where you have seen that you carry all of the Earth within you. You have seen that you have reincarnated over and over again and have moved into forgiveness, love, beauty, and understanding. It's not just forgiveness of the Earth, but forgiveness of yourself. It's a process of learning to forgive, to love again and to raise your brain from the animal state to purity. That's basically what happens. Human beings raise themselves each life into purity, into God beings. It takes time; it takes love, beauty, peace, understanding, and even some suffering before you can forgive all that and forgive yourself. You learn, you rise, and your brain develops from an animal consciousness to the Divine. You all carry the seeds of the Divine; you have to be watered, you have to be fed, you have to be nurtured, you have to be with those who are conscious and aware and can nurture you, enlighten you, and raise you. Every human being has the chance to become enlightened. It may take many lifetimes. It might take shorter lifetimes. It's different for everyone. That's why there will always be the Divine around. There will always be those who will get enlightened and will carry on to help humanity awaken. It's a big picture. It will take time. When you read this book, you just sit in your heart. Call the Absolute or the Divine or God. Whatever word you want to use, call it ten times. Ask for directions to awaken your being. Ask for the sleepy one inside to awaken, to learn, grow, love, uplift, care for others, and bring about peace in yourself and others in your world, in the trees, the ocean, the sky, and the stars. Go into the peace. Go into the place where the Divine can awaken you in a moment. It takes some time, it takes love, and it takes forgiveness—complete forgiveness, no matter what happens. This will happen to those who are ready. They will have enlightened experiences that they are everything. That they are love and beauty; they are nature, the stars, the moon, the sky, the wind, the rain, the oceans, the rivers and trees, the homes, the children, the grass, the Earth, and the moon. You know you are all of that in one moment. In that moment, you feel God in every cell in your body and you are light itself. This is very big. This is very special, but it can happen in time. It can happen. You will and can awaken.

Love is the key. Forgiveness of yourself and others is the key. Intelligence is the key, and raising your knowledge. Finding the peace in your heart to forgive all those who've ever hurt you, and to forgive yourself for anyone you've ever hurt. This is the beginning; and in the end, it's still the same. We love you all. We hope this book helps you. We hope you awaken. Call our names. Call the masters you find. Ask them for help. They will come. They are all being sent to help this planet awaken with love.

CHAPTER 4

The Absolute

Some people are on the Earth to relearn compassion and love and to open their hearts more. Different planets do different jobs. This planet is a planet of upliftments for all kinds of people to come back and open their hearts, consciousness, and awareness. So that's why we are calling through consciousness, love, and awareness. There are many different dimensions on this planet. Through this book, people will be called to their assignments, meaning many people forgot because when they came onto the Earth they did forget what their jobs were. You are learning so much from what the Earth is anyway; people forget they have a calling. So we're going to try to gather them again through this book. When they read it, they will remember, and they will contact us. People will be drawn that way. Not everybody, but the right ones who are supposed to.

The Absolute Speaks

So we are going to call the Absolute to come and speak and see what they have to say. Alright, hold on ... this is what I say in my prayer. "Dear beloved Absolute ... with great honoring, great caring, great love, and great joy we come to you to ask you to share some wisdom for this book…this book of love for humanity." OK, hold on now. The Absolute is speaking now … First I must say that the Absolute is just a word, and you have to use words to communicate. When we say "Absolute," we want people to realize that we are speaking from existence, way beyond anything you can imagine. We are giving instructions and knowledge to help this particular planet. When we say "the Absolute," it means we are calling forth information from … I don't know another word to say it … the Absolute. I don't know another word in English that can describe the immensity of love, knowledge, beauty, and upliftment for this planet. So we contact the Absolute which is so huge you can't even imagine. We are working with the Earth planet. Every planet has a position. Every planet has a job. Every planet has different upliftments, different consciousnesses, different levels of awakening, levels of caring, and levels of leaving the darkness to the light. It has many, many, many transformations. When we say "Absolute," we are saying we are giving information from the love of the Absolute which is all there is. That can be given in many different ways because your planet is at a particular level of consciousness, so you will receive knowledge for this planet that will be different than it may be for a different planet, you understand, so it's not all the same. Our agreement with the Council is to give this book to the Earth from the love of all there is, or the Absolute. There is great love for this planet. This planet is a great experiment because it is pretty free. People's levels of consciousness that arrive on this planet are slowly, slowly, for a long time, raising their consciousness, their awareness, their love, their brilliance, their compassion, their socialness, and many things. On your planet, you have the lowest of low and the highest of high, and not all planets are like that. Many planets are just in the middle. On some planets there are very high beings that are constantly working with all the universes.

There are also the planets that are lower-consciousness, so that's what we wanted to share with everyone. It's more complicated than you think. Your planet carries so many different dimensions and so many different levels of consciousness, awareness, languages, and heritages. You have the Japanese, the Chinese, the Greeks, the German, the English, the Spanish, and many other languages like the American Indian, and you have the French, and it just goes on and on ... all the languages and the different dimensions of people which all have different cultures. So it's quite remarkable, actually. This was a planet to see if all the different kinds of beings could live together. As you've seen over time, that was not always easy, and people had to learn that they were of love. They are not just animals, but they have animal energy that had been developed into what we call humans. The intelligence as a human being is at different levels, different consciousness, and different cultures so you have quite a job here on this Earth. Actually, so far, it's doing pretty good. The things that were put in place before this experiment was given were love and the heart. Everyone, no matter how good or bad they are on this Earth, has love implanted in them. Whether it is erupted or has been found or uplifted is another question. This planet has lasted so long because everyone was seeded with love. That doesn't mean they were love. It means they were seeded. Whether or not the seed exploded and opened is another story. That's where you have those who are not in a state capable of love as a presence of aliveness on the planet. Through many, many, many centuries and times, this planet has been uplifted and is still being uplifted. It's still growing, but it has sped up. Have you noticed? The things that still have to be addressed are all the different cultures, languages, and traditions. When the people came onto the Earth they were very primitive, and they were in all different places and different times. You can see how complicated it is. As communication and languages are understood, writings are given and Councils are gathered. We have seeded many new beings. Younger ones have been seeded with a lot more love than has been given to others, depending on the upliftment of their consciousness. Amritam was given great amounts of love because of her upliftment of her consciousness. So what I'm saying is that this happened naturally, but now we are infusing love and consciousness to those much faster so it doesn't take so long. The Councils of Divine Beings of love are trying to keep the planet raised in consciousness, love, compassion, and joy. Those who are not ready to raise their vibrations of consciousness will be taught and given beautiful gifts from Heaven to awaken their hearts and their knowledge to uplift them into higher consciousness. All this takes time in your timing, a lot of time. For us, it's not so long; but for you, ten years, hundreds of years, thousands of years is a lot. In our world that's not true. It's like this. (Oceana snaps their fingers.) Things happen quickly. If you've noticed, things have sped up a bit in the last eighty years. Think of all the new gifts of knowledge that have been given. People who were born were implanted with developing computers, this and that. With the babies who are born now and the children who are around twelve to fifteen years old, you'll see they are going to come up with even more grand upliftments for the planet, so that's very exciting. The soul worlds of the ancient ones and beyond (which I can't describe to you because it's too big) are very pleased with the planets right now. They are working with the cultures that hadn't developed properly. Ones that have animal mental problems of imbalance are still on your planet. In the future, everyone will slowly be uplifted into high consciousness with love and mental, physical, emotional, and spiritual balance. It's a big job. So there's a lot of beautiful things happening here and a lot of things that are happening in the background that your culture doesn't understand or know. I'm not sure I can tell everybody all of this yet, but we can give a feel of it. I'm making it really simple. It's more complicated than that, but you get the idea. So what I'm saying to you is that your planet is being uplifted, and you can even see that in every way. Those who are keeping it from the highest consciousness of a God planet will be given blessings that will raise them into higher consciousness. This is going to take some time. So this planet now is rising very beautifully into a high-consciousness place, wouldn't you say so? So, not only are there different masters and teachers going to be sent, like Master Sha (he's really helped in a lot of ways and brought consciousness), but slowly, slowly, there will be even more beautiful teachers being given in the immensity of giving love where people are just so touched that all the darkness that was in them dissolves. That hasn't happened yet, but it will. There will be great ones given to almost every country that is in a Council, and they will all be working together. At first they won't know it, but then we will give them the information. When that happens in the future, that Council will spread love, consciousness, and balance through everyone. There will be a particular kind of meditation that will be given to each culture. When they do the meditation, it will change any negativity or imbalance in the person. Cruelty in them or whatever is dark will be cleansed from them. I'm talking of the future here. This is not happening tomorrow. Eventually, when that all occurs, this planet will be like Heaven. Not to say exactly how you imagine Heaven, but it will be a planet of upliftment, purity, and love. There will be no cruelty, there will be no wars, and there will be no imbalances in their brains. There will be no mental illness, there will be no anger and no imbalances of mental problems. Eventually, this will be a pure place of Heaven. That is what it is slowly moving to. The same thing happened to the heavenly places that are in existence. Then you are saints. Even now, there are saints here from the upliftments the masters that have come gave to them. So it's a big, big, big picture. It started with all the gurus who have come to your planet, especially since you developed TVs, phones, and whatever you call them. Communication skills have tremendously transformed the planet, and there will be more. People will be gathered together as if they are right next to each other. Slowly, slowly, in some of the governments on the Earth that cannot be transformed, yet different ways will be approached for them. I can't say because it's not happened yet. Eventually, anything that is out of balance will be balanced. To bring those who are ready into pure balance, and to eventually teach ones who need balance and new knowledge, there will be blessings given. This planet is in the limelight of God's arms, hands, being, and soul to raise its consciousness, its love, its abundance, and its beauty. It's being raised to house saints, angels, beings of love, beings of consciousness, and beings of creation. When, for example, somebody discovers how to build a car, that is the person who was seeded with that. Henry Ford had a different kind of brain. He had a different mission. He had a different ability to bring; and if you think about it, cars brought people together because they couldn't travel. So everything is being given from the high beings of light to this planet to do the same kind of thing. I'm not only talking about cars but about uplifting the planet so it is a heavenly planet. That's where it is going. That's what it was chosen for. It's not going to happen overnight. If you people who read this book understand that, and understand this book of love, that love is beyond existence, you'll know that what I mean is that love is the healer, the Creator. When you say "the Absolute," it's even the Absolute, so love is the Absolute. Love is the Creator, love is all there is and all there ever shall be. It's all one presence. So, when you call in God—like you call God, or the highest of high, or all there is—there is a presence of light. It is very huge and very big. As we are sitting here, Councils are sitting in the room. The presence of the Absolute energy fields are around us. They take the information I have given into the book and into the world and actually give me advice for things to say and communicate. So you can see this is a new beginning to help your humanity understand the big picture. Those who were not treated properly will slowly, slowly be healed through love and caring. This will be a planet sort of like what you all imagine as Heaven, but it takes time. That's where you are going; that's where you are heading to. Now, how are you going to get there? That would be the next chapter. How are you going to get there? You are going to get there by understanding, by the Councils that are sending enlightened souls to be born here— many, many, many of which are going to bring balance, love, peace, and harmony to this planet. How lucky are you all who are still here and have gotten love and joy but still have confusion and darkness there? Everyone has a little of that on the planet. So, slowly, slowly, you will all be transformed with teachers and masters like Master Sha, like Osho, like other masters who are here: gurus in India, gurus in different places, and ancient ones in the Himalayas who are holding the space and keeping the balance on the Earth. There are many of them, just so you know. There are Councils that happen in the Himalayas and in different places. You will never find them, so don't go out searching, because you will not be allowed. Only those who are assigned can ever be there. So just get to know this to give you hope, to give you the upliftment you need to bring forth your own higher consciousness. Through meditation, through caring, through love, through forgiveness, through caring for others; being responsible for others, responsible for your Earth in each way, to keep uplifting and gathering love ... beings of love, beings of love, and beings of love. That will take some time, though. So we are very happy to write this book. Hopefully, it will inspire you all to really go into meditation, really come to classes, and really move to forgiveness ... forgiveness of pain, suffering, and hurt; forgiveness of yourself. This will bring you into a higher-consciousness place and will transform you, your family, your planet, your food, your animals, and your ability to raise higher and higher intelligence to bring peace, love, and harmony here. It will also allow you to develop ways to reach cultures in your world that you haven't heard of yet. For example, when you hadn't heard of your cell phone or TVs, and you didn't even have radios, you only had Morse code. So slowly, slowly, there will be more ways and much faster ways to contact. You'll find that someday there will be planes that go very quickly so you don't spend five hours in a plane to get somewhere. Your transportation, your abilities of flying, and your abilities of communicating are going to be so much faster. This will all help the planet rise in love, consciousness, and beauty. This is very important for meditation, celebration, and kindness. If you are lucky to have more money than others, it's very important for those of you who've been blessed to help humanity gather together to uplift your consciousness into pure love, forgiveness, joy, and balancing as you learn meditation. Balance as you are keeping the balance of the left and right hemispheres in the brain. That's a lot that I just said. I know everybody has wanted this book to come. So that is why we are doing this. You have so many different cultures here, and some of them are still warring. We are working on that because this planet has been upgraded to be raised as a high-consciousness, heavenly place. This will be seen pretty soon in the next twenty or thirty years. Slowly, we'll see the planet rising and rising. Those who will be here will be part of uplifting and love, consciousness, joy, and forgiveness, forgiveness, forgiveness. I can't say that enough. Forgiveness, forgiveness, forgiveness of each other and yourself. That's your magic word. As I'm sitting here, they are saying, "Why not call the book *Love and Forgiveness*, because without those two things, this planet will not transform." Forgiveness and love, however you want to say it. It's what people need, because it can't go anywhere without that.

CHAPTER 5

Communication, Love, and Understanding

This chapter is of the heart. We are going to share how this world will come together. The only way is love, the heart, forgiveness, joy, peace, celebration, meditation ... you can see it's a big job. One of the most important things that needs to happen on your planet is communication and understanding of different cultures. Part of the problem is that you all have different languages of love, communication, and understanding of countries/realities. One thing that everyone needs to know is that it doesn't have to take that long, but because of egos and imbalanced brains, it's taking so long for your world to be a heavenly place. It is being uplifted, and the more you all love, the more you understand, the more you celebrate, the more you help each other, the more you open your hearts and souls to the light, the more your planet will be uplifted. I was speaking about communicating to the cultures on the Earth. One thing we would like to have happen when the book is printed, if possible, is that each book is written in the language of each country. That way, everybody will get it. We want to translate it in all languages. So this book of love is very important. Without love, this world wouldn't be here at all. Your world is in such a situation at this time, including every state in America and every place in Europe and in the whole world, where there are people who are conscious and alive and living in human form. Now there are smaller places where there are people who are conscious and alive, but they are on a very small world and they live more primitively than you; not like hundreds of years ago, but still primitively. So there are many, many, many levels of human beings that are here and many levels of consciousness. There are many levels of intelligence and many beings that are sent here with higher consciousness, awareness, love, and compassion to learn from this Earth. There are those who are very wise, very intelligent, and very advanced that are here. Also there are some lower energies that cause havoc and confusion. That's how it is on this Earth. Hopefully, we're trying to reach each European country. Each country has a person, maybe one or two, who can channel and bring forth information like Amritam does and like I will do. And slowly, in time, we will call them together, and that will help humanity because people will listen to the other channels. These are the women or men who will bring the information together, but nobody knows this yet. And we have not contacted everyone at this time. It's just beginning.

CHAPTER 6

The Soul World

My dearest ones, as you all know, you are all seeded from the Absolute. So that means you are all one. For some of you that will be very disturbing. What's going to happen is that not everybody is seeded with the information in their whole world. So this book is the beginning of that. There will be other books, and the right people will receive the books. It could be that many people will buy the book and read the book, but it will be just interesting for them. There are people whom the book was calling who have been seeded with information and pieces of understanding of the soul world and the Earth and all the things that can happen here. Slowly, as you've seen, the world is being uplifted. Things can slowly be balanced, if possible. It's a little difficult in the universe because there are a lot of energies going on everywhere in the universe, so to speak. Because of the presence of the ancient ones (I don't mean ancient ones from your world, but the ancient ones from existence that are in charge of keeping the Earth and other planets that have life on it in balance), we're trying to do that with the understanding and with people who are being seeded to be born here with information and with knowledge. Twenty or thirty years ago, there were the children who were born and are coming into knowledge now. They are remembering.

There are different people through the timings who were seeded with information; and then, whatever that was for them, that has gone away. They were just done. Their job with us and the soul world was done; and if they are to be called back, they'll find us. We don't go out after them. They'll come to us if we need more people. A lot has happened from when I came onto the Earth here to speak. It's been thirty years since she started channeling me. So much has happened in the world, and things can happen much more quickly now. Your planet is slowly becoming a bit more advanced and has higher consciousness. Still, because this Earth has the lowest of low and highest of high consciousness, it's always been a problem. Slowly, what's happening is that, because of the ability to communicate to all the different kinds of people and languages and heritages, it's easier now because things are being more peaceful. So much has been developed. So much intelligence has been given to the planet, for many people and young babies who were born thirty years ago are now thirty, and they have information now too. They have ways of communicating that weren't around. That was half the problem. People are more intelligent. They are looking for more upliftments of their being. Not just in America, but in every country. What we did was give in the huge world, of all there is, seeded babies and children to come onto the Earth. They were very intelligent; not lower consciousness, but higher consciousness. As you see, everyone's a bit more aware, more conscious, and more loving; and you still have the confusion and dark energy, but not at the rate you had before. All that is being changed in time. So the reason the book is coming out now, and wasn't before, is because people weren't ready for it. Now there are intelligent beings who are fifteen years old and onward who have been given ancient knowledge. Things will slowly pop. This piece will come together, and that piece will come together, and your world will move into higher consciousness and be more peaceful. There's so much love that is coming your way, not just from the inner part of your Earth because of the ancient ones that are here, but there are a lot of loving beings who are sending love and healing and knowledge to individuals who are seeded on the planet. I'm trying to explain that, in the universe of this place, you are being bombarded with love, knowledge, and information to keep the planet in harmony and balance. Without that, there was going to be things that were not going to be good on the Earth and in the universe. It would affect everyone. So what we did in the soul world was we gathered all the beings together and came up with sending love, light, and knowledge to everyone who was born. Even if they were grown, they would get knowledge through writing; or suddenly, they would have an epiphany about something. So what's happening is that we are all coming together as oneness, and that's really always been our message. Those who are ancient and who have experience with meditation and who have gifts from the Absolute to remind them of who they are slowly, slowly will all come together. As this book comes into the Earth, you who are reading this book are being called because you are seeded with knowledge of awareness, love, consciousness, and better ways to run things in the world, to create a space of intelligence, lovingness, and caring. So, in the universe, we are uplifting the Earth from lower consciousness to higher consciousness. When that is occurring, beings are born here with great knowledge. So you will see in the next hundred years that this planet will be a very high-consciousness planet and a very loving planet. For your Earth needs to be balanced in the universe with love so it will keep everything in balance in the universe. This means that if the Earth moves off into darkness, it affects everybody (or any planet that moves into the darkness; it's not just the Earth). So we had to shift the energy here and send higher consciousness here through babies, people being born to bring knowledge to the Earth. What's happening on the Earth now is the higher consciousness that surrounds your Earth. There's consciousness that's in the Earth that's medium and lower. There's higher consciousness of beings that are sent to Earth to teach them and uplift their souls, to bring a rising of awareness and coming together in the middle. So your Earth is balanced; but it hasn't been balanced, because you had low consciousness, medium consciousness, and higher consciousness. This is difficult especially for the higher consciousness and the more aware consciousness. The lower consciousness has to be seeded and raised from animal conditioning to higher human conditioning. That is happening here, but not as quickly as it was supposed to; but your planet has become a lot more peaceful overall. It has been happening out of knowledge that was sent down to the Earth through a couple of ways. Some in the universal awareness group saw what was happening on this planet. The lower consciousness, the wars, the imbalance of the brains, it realized it had to be seeded through births and people having children and things like that. Those seeds were uplifted, and your planet was seeded with higher-consciousness beings than what had been given here before. You can see it in your planet if you look back one hundred or two hundred years ago; it's not like the same kind of people here anymore. They are full of knowledge and awareness. Their brains are working better, they are ancient. Your planet has been seeded with ancient beings to raise its consciousness so that it raised the Earth and the other planets that were around that needed the same things that were seeded. So you're rising, and there are three or four other planets rising. In the higher realms of everything, they are holding the space to lift everything into love, everything into peace, everything into awareness and consciousness. They are rising in a way that everyone feels the sense of God inside of them. That wasn't happening before. It happens, but not enough. It's not only happening on this planet but on other planets that were not rising quickly enough. So it's a very big story ... a very big story. It's very important for people to understand forgiveness, love, peace, and consciousness. So slowly, slowly, in the ancient, ancient, ancient ways that we can't talk about that are so ancient and so advanced the whole planet will eventually get balanced in the center of love, peace, and harmony. That's why you are getting teachers and masters who are bringing that knowledge to your Earth. There are more than one. That's why Master Sha and other ones bring love, peace, and harmony. It's the key; the keywords are love, peace, and harmony for your planet. I'm saying it's rising, it's shifting, it's changing, because you're being seeded with intelligence that people didn't have yet. In the soul world there isn't time. It's just happening, and really, I know the answer seems strange to everybody, but it's about love. The more that there are balanced families, balanced parents, and balanced children who just focus on love, more and more it will rise. That's my message, and there are things that can happen here on the Earth that will be in balance. More and more love ... that's why I'm writing the book! You have got to focus on love, you've got to focus on love. That's what will balance your planet, other planets, and your universe. That is your antidote. Whenever you give medicine, what do you call it? Your antidotes are love and forgiveness. It's not that hard. Those who have been hurt have to forgive. That's part of their upliftment. It's part of their consciousness, part of their awakening. They have to move to forgiveness, and forgive themselves and forgive others. It's a big job. It's a spiritual job. In the universe in the soul world, the Councils are coming together to help raise the consciousness, love, awareness, and peace in each person. So what we've been thinking about doing is seeding the seeds of love, awareness, consciousness, intelligence, and a sense of peace and harmony in every person who is born. You can't really say they are new, but they have been uplifted. So they are the same ones coming back and forth sometimes, but they are uplifted in love, peace, and harmony. It's what's in their cells; in their brains; in their DNA, RNA, and everything in the body. It's in seeded with love, peace, and harmony. So the new ones coming are going to bring that slowly, slowly through everything on the planet. The trees, the flowers—just by the presence of the energy of love, peace, and harmony—is in them, balanced in them. The right and left hemispheres in the brain are balanced, so eventually, in time, you are going to have a very high-consciousness, aware, peaceful planet. That's what we are working on. To bring that to this planet, it's a big job. It's going to take time, but it's started. It actually started after the last big war. Then, in the soul world, we said, "OK, we've got to fix this, you know, this is not good." Since that time there have been many, many new beings seeded with love, peace, and harmony. I'm just using that word so people understand that it's in their cells. That's what they've come here to do. They don't even know what they are doing. You'll see it in the children's faces, you'll see it in the schools, you'll see new teachers coming. Slowly, slowly, we will try to balance and bring higher consciousness to other countries. We're here in America, but other countries are also being seeded. We have to do it in every country or every part of your Earth. You call them countries, but we call them just other pieces to heal, like putting a puzzle together. So this Earth is being seeded with love, peace, and harmony. This will take time; it's not going to happen in a day. It's going to take many years; but eventually, this planet will be almost like a heavenly planet which will be transformed through time, through meditations, and through the energy coming through the Divine Ones in all the universes blessing you and your Earth to come home to its Source. Those who rise in consciousness, love, and caring, and listen to the Source of the enlightened ones that are speaking to them, will change it. That's what will happen. That's why we're writing this book. We are calling people who are seeded with this information, even if they don't know it. They'll suddenly come to a lecture, or read the book, and they'll say, "Oh, you should read this book, and read that ..." And slowly, the right people will gather together. In time, I will come and speak about the book to them as the book is spread around. It's not just Oceana here doing this. There are many other awakened masters like us working through other people in different countries who also get this information. They may also write a different kind of book but similar. Slowly, we are trying to seed England, and seed Germany, and this country, and this one, and this one, and this one, and this one. Like we're implanting stars of light into people who will get this information and help create it. People will come together. It's just beginning. So it's good the book will get out.

───── CHAPTER 7 ─────
Love and Forgiveness

Love and forgive. The biggest thing that needs to happen on your Earth is forgiveness. This is so important. It is where all the teaching must go. Forgiveness of yourself, forgiveness of God, of the Earth, of the governments, of the people, of the dark, of the light and of love, forgiveness of the self, forgiveness of mistakes, forgiveness of unintelligence. This is what most of it is all about. For, without forgiveness, your Earth cannot rise. But you must start small. If you look around in every country, what would be the antidote for the disease, the anger, the killing, the hurt, the mental disturbance? It's all about forgiveness. First of all, beloveds, each and every one of you have been in a state of rising. From the very seeded moment God gave you life in your seed in this timing, many of you have reincarnated back and forth. Each time you were seeded with light. Each time you were seeded with knowledge. Each time you were seeded with consciousness. Each time you were seeded with learning through lifetimes of learning and experiences of love, joy, sadness, grief, misunderstanding, and lower consciousnesses as you were rising. Many of you now have been given and seeded just pure love, and you are being balanced and raised into higher consciousness. The whole planet is slowly being seeded with love, higher consciousness, and forgiveness. Now, what is forgiveness? Forgiveness is what raises your planet. Forgiveness is what raises your consciousness. Forgiveness is what brings love, abundance, peace, and consciousness. What makes it possible for you to rise is forgiveness. When you forgive anything, your heart and your being are full of pure love when forgiveness happens. Then that moves out of you and into your world, and it brings intelligence to your brain. Forgiveness is the key to awakening. Awakening is enlightenment. It means you are in a state of pure forgiveness for all and everything. When you move to that state, you are consumed with forgiveness of yourself, of people, of the Earth, of planets, forgiveness of all there is and all that shall happen. You are then slowly, slowly raised to enlightenment. Without forgiveness, nothing can happen, for you're in a process of transformation. When you get to the place of forgiveness, understanding, and love, you explode with forgiveness for yourself and all there is. You are never the same again. You are in a state of love, peace, harmony, and light. This is what will raise your planet; your awareness will bring beautiful, beautiful high consciousness to this planet. There will be a sense of peace when you forgive everything, a sense of light, a sense of intelligence, and an awareness that you are one with all things. When you experience that enlightened moment, everything explodes within you and you rise to the purity of love, peace, and harmony. You just don't say it; you are it. When that happens, your planet begins to transform into this high space of purity and love. Forgiveness is very important. Forgiveness is the keyword for this planet and all planets to awaken. Only through forgiveness will purity transform and create this planet and all beings into a state of light, love, abundance, harmony, and joy. Wow ... that is the kind of planet you are creating now. This will not only help all and everyone to rise, but in the universe, it will bring harmony as well. Still full of love, full of light, allowing yourself to forgive opens all doors to the Divine; to peace; to joy; to celebration; to laughing, loving, and truly caring for each other. It's so important to celebrate. It's important not to go into the gloom and doom. It's important to see it in a brand-new way. We're not going to go back and go over all the mistakes that have been made. We have to honor them. We have to learn from them. Then we move forward. The biggest problem is that people who are financially not good have the hardest time. They have to move to forgiveness. This is the biggest and most important of all: forgiveness on all levels. This is why your Earth has had so much trouble. It's difficult because the human being is emotion, because the human being loves, the human being cares, the human being loses balance in the left and right hemispheres in the brain. So, if you are annoyed at someone, it's important that you don't allow that annoyance to disturb you. You just forgive them. The next thing after this love is that you have to move to forgiveness of yourself, God, everybody, parents, family, and lifetimes. The world isn't bad or erratic or crazy. It's just that you have to allow yourself to forgive yourself and others. It doesn't mean you let them hurt you. It just means you forgive. You still don't allow people to mistreat you. This is an Earth that is not an enlightened Earth. It is rising, it is growing, but it is not enlightened. There are planets that are enlightened, but we will bring forth many helpers. There are many conscious people here on the planet who are balancing your Earth. I saw something yesterday with Amritam. There was a boy in a swimming pool who lost his mother. Amritam got out of the pool, and another man did too. Those two people were conscious human beings. The rest were sleeping. He picked the boy up, and the boy's daddy saw him, and there was peace again for the little child. But I was watching. I saw so many people who were just asleep. They didn't even hear the little boy crying. They didn't even feel the suffering in his heart.

These are people who are sleeping. We have to wake them up. We have to wake them up to love, to responsibility, to caring, to not being afraid to be the loving ones who are in there to come out. These are the problems on the Earth. People have forgotten love. It's coming and being given again. Higher-consciousness beings are being brought here to write books; to give talks; to awaken those who need to rise, who need to meditate, who need to love, who need to serve, who need to heal their own problems. How to heal them? Just like when you go to pick up the little boy who is crying. You love him and the next person, and the daddy finds him, and then there's a celebration of consciousness, love, caring, and awakening. The whole world starts to rise in pure love and responsibility which is responding in the here and now. Responding to the boy to help him so he doesn't get hurt. Responding with love; responding with action; responding with caring; responding with peace, joy, and laughter. Bringing everyone to a higher awareness. That is what's happening on your Earth. They will be brought consciousness, forgiveness, and awakening to higher brains. Those who are ready for transformation and for love, who are full of love and are responsible ... responding in the here and now with love. They are aware; they are caring; they want to help humanity, help education, and help the planet. They want to stop all the destruction. They're all coming to your Earth so that it can eventually be an enlightened planet. That is what's happening. Those of you who are ready—and I'm saying you can be ready if you choose—you'll be on a planet of enlightenment. So it's a process. It doesn't happen overnight; but without a beginning, it cannot happen. The beginning started long ago, but now it is rising quicker and faster, and that's important.

Meditation/Visualization: Forgiveness and Service

Everybody, just get comfortable and just close your eyes. Get comfortable so your spine is able to let the kundalini move. Take a nice, deep breath ... a really nice, deep breath, relaxing your shoulders ... another nice, deep breath ... and another beautiful breath. You say inside, "Dear, beloved soul of mine. I love you. I care about you. I am in great gratitude for my life. The soul within me, that I am, you are. We have grown beautifully, we have learned, we have changed, we've suffered, we've been hurt, but we kept walking forward with our heart. We just kept moving with our light. We learned to forgive ourselves. We learned to forgive others. We learned to celebrate life; to celebrate the sun, the moon, the trees, the rivers, the forest, and the mountains. We've learned to appreciate this life we have. We've learned to forgive ourselves for mistakes. We've learned to forgive those who have hurt us. We've taken responsibility for our life." Responsibility is responding in the here and now with love for yourself and others. When you do that, the Divine opens their heart to the beautiful soul you are. The beautiful, wise one that served humanity with your heart, with your joy, with money, with beauty, with painting, with laughing, dancing, looking at the stars, helping others ... this is your life. A life of meditation, a life of service to humanity and yourself, a life to give and receive and be a balanced light of God. As you sit there, dear one, thank your soul and thank yourself for your life, your joy, and even your losses, because they have gotten you to grow and transform. Just love again. Just keep loving again and again ... remembering the stars, the sky, the rivers, the oceans, and the light you are. You are all of that. When you find what you love to do, do it with all your heart. Forgive all those people who have ever hurt you, and forgive yourself if you've ever hurt anyone else. Every morning, when you wake up, you say, "Dear Divine, thank you for this life; thank you for allowing me to grow, to learn, to live, and to transform. I can't wait to experience more joy and more love for all." Allow yourself to laugh, allow yourself to give to yourself. If you are always giving, giving, giving, you leave yourself not receiving. That's why we take people to the beautiful hot springs, so they laugh, heal their bodies, take care of themselves, and help each other. Transformation is not always sitting and meditating. It is living your life with joy and service, and healing your body and heart. Allow yourself to create, and allow yourself to transform. So, now as you sit there, dear one, thank your soul, thank the Divine, thank God, thank all your teachers; and remember you are love, you come from love, come from growing, transforming; and keep going forward. Allow your ideas, your dreams, and your hopes to happen. Talk to people, meet people, open up, and dance in the world with love, happiness, and joy. Alright, dear ones, we thank you for this night, we thank you for your time with us. We love to share our heart; it is a gift, and you are a gift to us. With love from Oceana and the Twenty-Four and Amritam, please enjoy your life. We love you, we honor you, and we care for you. I ring the bell, calling all the ancient ones, all the people longing to be happy again, all the people who need meditation, and all the ones who haven't found us yet. So we can help hundreds of people to remember that they are light, they are love, they are already abundant, and they can give to other human beings with joy and happiness. Love, love, light, light, light, peace, peace, peace, peace. We love you; we care for you; we send healing to you; we send joy, abundance, and creativity to continue your lives with new ideas. OK, have a beautiful night.

CHAPTER 8

Raising Your Consciousness

For those of you who are new to meditation, awareness of the soul, and awareness of your spiritual self and are just learning meditation and just getting into what enlightenment is and learning about different masters who have been on the planet; and for those of you who are just starting your journey, we want to give some information to you so you can start a new journey. There are many beautiful, enlightened masters on the planet right now, but there needs to be more. It's part of this planet's upliftment, so every one of you who is curious, who is longing to find the Divine, God, or their inner selves and have had not-so-great lives on the planet, it means you were sent here to raise your vibration, to look bigger, and to find a teacher on the Earth who can uplift your soul standing. Your soul standing is consciousness as well, and this raises you to find the Divine. Many of you, because you don't have that training, just long to be with God or what your heart is pulling you and your soul to. So we are sending different teachers to gather many of you who have not had the chance to learn about God, about meditation, about uplifting your awareness, about your consciousness, about your brain, about forgiveness, about learning how to raise your vibration on the Earth. So this is a planet of learning, and we are sending higher-consciousness presences because it's also a planet that is slowly moving into an enlightened planet. This means that all the people who will live here will be enlightened. That has not happened here yet. Many of you will find this book; your souls are leading you to this book. Your souls are longing to be free, longing to understand what consciousness is, what God is, what is right, what is wrong, and learning forgiveness. Many, many, many of your people on this Earth must go to forgiveness of themselves, forgiveness of the planet, forgiveness of teachers, forgiveness of leaders, forgiveness of the unawareness, and forgiveness of yourself and of mistakes in this life and other lives so you can slowly move into a true space of understanding that you are developing into a higher-consciousness person. That leads you into a higher awareness; a higher brain; a higher ability to forgive, to love, to celebrate life, to raise your awareness; to long to be free on your Earth; to help your family, your children, and humanity. So we sent people here to do that. To learn, to make mistakes, to forgive themselves, and to find their hearts. We are there to help those who are sincere; those who are longing; those who are willing to forgive hurt, pain, grief, and sadness. Know that this is karma, and through forgiveness, you are uplifting yourself to consciousness, awareness, and even a space of purity and enlightenment. Without forgiveness, nothing can happen for you or anyone. Forgiveness of people who have hurt you or forgiveness of yourself; the biggest thing on this planet is the word forgiveness. It needs to happen in every country on this planet, and it is the key to an enlightened planet. It is the key to opening your heart, to opening love, to opening peace. This is the key; this is the key, dear ones: for you to go inside, sit in your heart, forgive yourself, forgive those who've hurt you, forgive your mind, forgive the other beings on the Earth. Forgive them, God, for they do not know. That is Jesus's message. That is the major message that Jesus gave to this Earth, and it has been almost forgotten. It should be everywhere. In all the countries, and for the governments, read this: forgive them, for they do not know. That means you can forgive yourself; you can forgive others who are imbalanced, and help the imbalanced people to be loved, cured, and healed. Slowly, that is happening on your planet. There are people who are helping and working with people who are mentally not well. Things went wrong. They were not balanced. Believe it or not, love can heal mental illness, depression, grief, and loneliness. Through love, through awareness, through consciousness, and through forgiveness, they will be uplifted. Eventually, you are sent to an enlightened planet. Now some of you are already there, but you were also sent to this planet which is not an enlightened planet. Some of you in enlightenment—whether you are a teacher or just a regular person—were sent here to help the Earth rise in more and more consciousness. It's a big story, you know, so I am sharing as much as I can for now to get the people who find this book to think bigger, to meditate, to find a teacher, to get serious about their lives and forgiveness. Without it, nothing can happen. So I will do a visualization for forgiveness. Alright, everybody, just close your eyes. Go inside and say, "Dear soul of mine. Awaken within me. I am in deep gratitude for the soul I am. I am here to go inside and forgive myself, and all others in past lives and in this life, whom I have hurt or who have hurt me. This way, I can forgive my own mistakes in this life; and in the future, I will be in a place of forgiveness of all that I have done to hurt others and all that others have done to hurt me." That is what you have to say. Those of you who move into the forgiveness practice, you truly have to go in and forgive those who have hurt you, and forgive yourself whom you have hurt. This takes time because the mind is slow to get that this is so important and that you are still in a process of learning. There are many through your lifetimes who were not intelligent, were not trained, or were almost in the animal conditioning, but that's no longer happening to you now. Now you are on a conscious planet that is slowly, slowly rising. It is not an enlightened planet, but it does have more light than most planets. It has more love, more forgiveness, and more knowledge. Slowly, slowly, it is rising. This planet has made huge mistakes, just like other planets, with wars and bombs and atomic things. All this is negative. All this is important to forgive yourself if you've been involved. Forgive the world and the teachers and parents who were unconscious and almost animal-like. This is a problem, but it is being healed, and you have all had to rise from low consciousness. Not everyone, because we have always sent enlightened ones to help this planet rise in purity and mental imbalance. Maybe they were not trained in love, respect, and consciousness. Many of you were hurt by parents who were unconscious. That is changing on your Earth. Slowly, slowly, new and beautiful beings will be born here. This planet is slowly rising as an enlightened planet. It has a long way to go. That's why I'm writing the book. That is why, in the soul world, there will be others who are saying, "Hey … forgiveness!" We are sending light to your brains. We are sending knowledge to your hearts. We are sending forgiveness so those of you who are ready to rise, who are in forgiveness of themselves and others, can rise into states of enlightenment. That's what's happening on this planet. So, dear ones, please take this book seriously; please go inside, please ask your soul if you want to stay in darkness or would like to rise in enlightenment. You have a chance to do that on this planet. Slowly, we will be sending more and more enlightened ones to help you rise. That is why you came to this planet: to forgive, to become conscious, to be aware, to learn what love is, and to uplift your intelligence in your brain and your soul. This is very important and necessary. If you ignore all this, you will once again be in a dark place. You don't want that. You want a light place. You want love, you want meditation, you want enlightened ones to help your soul rise. That is why you are here on this planet. We are here to help, and many others are, too. It's very, very important that you forgive. So, now, everybody who's reading this book, sit and close your eyes. I will give you a beautiful meditation.

Meditation/Visualization: Forgiveness

So, dear ones, close your eyes, and find a beautiful space. Maybe it is in nature, maybe it is in a beautiful space in your home, or you go to the forest, or you go on a walk where you sit and you feel peace. You feel love, and you feel safe and relaxed. So, first of all, just close your eyes. Become comfortable, and listen to the hum ... hum ... hum ... hum... hum ... hum. Lift your eyes upward, and take a deep breath. (Oceana breathes in deeply three times.) Relax your body and relax your heart. Sit with your feet flat on the ground. Feel every part of your body relaxing. Call your soul. "Dear soul of mine, awaken within me. For we will meditate with love. I love myself, I love my soul, I love the Earth, I love all those who've helped me in this life. I am going inside to call forth the soul of the light that God has given me." As you sit there, visualize this beautiful being in golden light sitting in front of you. You call the golden light teacher to come. "Dear golden light teacher, please come and sit with me." You say it three times. "Dear golden light teacher, please sit with me. Dear golden light teacher, please sit with me." You sit before the being. Even if you can't see them, they are there. You take three deep breaths (Oceana takes three deep breaths), and you relax your body. You let go, and you feel the being of light sitting in front of you. Golden rays are surrounding you ... a bubble of golden rays of light. You relax. You put your hand on your heart, and you say, "I love my soul. I love my heart. I forgive myself for all those I've ever hurt, and I forgive those who've ever hurt me. From deep inside, I call forth the love, I call forth the Divine, and the ancient ones to sit with me; and I feel their presence. I thank them from my heart for loving me, for forgiving me, and for coming to uplift my consciousness." Then you relax and feel their presence, and you close your eyes if they are not closed. You sit and feel the hum. You feel the peace, you feel the heart, you feel your consciousness, and you feel the life force of God with you. You put your hand on your heart, and you say, "Dear soul of my heart, dear soul of the Divine, dear soul of God ... thank you for your gifts, thank you for your forgiveness. I also forgive all those who've hurt me, and I forgive myself for those whom I've hurt. Now I just sit in peace ... in the hum ... om ... om ... om ... om." Then feel this golden light come from the heavens and surround your body. You feel the love, you feel the peace ... you are one. Om ... om ... om ... love, love, love, forgiveness, forgiveness, forgiveness, peace, peace, peace, joy, joy, joy. You take three deep breaths, and you go inside. Put your hand on your heart. Thank your heart, thank God, thank yourself, and sit with love, peace, and harmony. Love, peace, and harmony. Love, peace, and harmony. Love, peace, and harmony ... whoosh ... (Oceana makes a sound ... whoosh)!

CHAPTER 9

Healing of the Heart

In the soul world we have many different committees to help keep the Earth balanced. We send different souls to the Earth that are higher souls, higher consciousness to be born here, masters with very important intelligence given to them. In different governments we've given higher consciousness. We thought this might bring balance to the Earth. There are so many souls that have been born, but things happened, and they did not use their powers properly. They did not remember they came to help, not to create more problems. So that's kind of what happens sometimes. We are now sending and being much more careful about beings of light that are born here, but they look normal, just like everyone. They have certain knowledge given to their brains to help bring balance to the mental, physical, and emotional bodies and balance to the Earth to bring it from an animal Earth to a highly enlightened planet. That's a big job. It's a shift and a change, a removal of different levels of souls to other planets to continue to grow and learn. That is what is happening to your planet. It's being uplifted to an enlightened planet. We have sent many beautiful masters, like Jesus and many others, to help this planet be uplifted. Each country has its own rules. We have to make sure the right person is born, and the right parents are there, and the right schools, and so on. To bring uplifted people who are beyond their parents (let's say just that) and have brilliant minds, tremendous hearts, consciousness, and love. That is what we are trying to do now. I'm not saying it's been done. I'm saying we're trying, and it has had some success; but now it needs to happen because there will be more and more enlightened children being born on your Earth. Slowly, slowly, that will shift and change and bring higher consciousness to your planet. Energy will shift and change. Love will start permeating, and everything will start moving into balance. There might be some shifts and changes and shakes here and there, but not like there has been. Our idea is to bring this planet into being an enlightened planet. New ones will be born here, and it will be created as a beautiful Garden of Eden, of love. That's our job. That's what we're trying to do here. That's why this book is out. That's why it's very important for people to really, really open their hearts of love, meditate, and find the teachers that we're going to be sending to help you go into higher awareness and higher consciousness. Use the brain that you will be receiving, and the caring you will be receiving, that will uplift you and your family and your country by just being in a state of love. The auric field around the Earth will also help and transform that. We're sending people to come here with higher consciousness, abilities, and love. They will help slowly, slowly bring balance here. It's already started, but it's going to take time.

Visualization for Healing of the Heart

Beloved ones, this is Oceana, and I am going to give a meditation on healing the heart. I know that those who find this book will be longing for their hearts to open, their beauty to come forth, and their joy to erupt within and around themselves. This brings love, happiness, abundance, working together and playing together, giving each other ways to rise through meditation, through love, through living in harmony, and through each person being given a way to help the Earth and be seeded. OK, dear ones, just close your eyes, and relax … know that you are loved. Know that you are cared for, and know that you have chosen to come to the Earth. You are all being seeded, or were seeded, with knowledge to help this planet become an enlightened planet. Each of you were given the seeds of knowledge, the seeds of love, the seeds of peace and harmony, the seeds of joy, and the seeds of abundance to bring this planet into balance and uplift it to a higher-consciousness state where everyone works as one. Where there is love, peace, and harmony, and where people are trained and have meditation in their hearts, are all coming together as one and full of love for these people with higher consciousness. They are brought to this Earth to send and bring higher consciousness to the Earth. The planet will be uplifted into light, into meditation, into caring, into responsibility, into healing each other, into being given new ways to bring this planet into being a holy planet. One with love, joy, and happiness. And everyone who comes to this Earth will be taken care of, and they will rise into light, rise into joy, rise into abundance, rise into caring for each other, rise into dancing in the light with gods. You are going to be a very special planet, Earth. Those who come here are being given orders on how to bring the planet into its highest consciousness possible. Those who are here will be easily brought up quickly into awakening and into consciousness, into caring, into abundance, joy, and healing this planet, healing each country, healing the whole planet and each person coming together in oneness. Each will have a gift to bring balance to the Earth, and then there will not be any more wars. This is going to take some time, but that's your future. There will be no more wars. There will be love, peace, harmony, upliftment, joy, and human beings who are balanced mentally, physically, emotionally, and spiritually. They will know that they came from God. They will know it, they will see it, and they will be assigned jobs. They will all come together as a much higher consciousness, much higher awareness, much higher knowledge in their brains, and this planet will be so beautiful. There will be no more wars. There will be no more suffering. Everyone will be seeded with higher consciousness, higher awareness, and higher abilities, and everyone will help each other because they have humanity in their hearts, they have love in their hearts, they have knowledge to heal the planet. Slowly, slowly, this will be a very special and very, very important planet because it will also help balance your universe. This is what we're hoping for. This is what we would like to have happen. Transformation by light, joy, happiness, abundance, and caring; deep caring, deep responsibility, knowingness that they are one with the Divine and that they are coming here to the Earth to bring the Divine and the light of God to this planet that has been trying to be uplifted. It will not happen in one day, but it will happen slowly, slowly. The children who will be born will be very uplifted, the parents will be uplifted, everyone will bring a piece of knowledge to the planet to keep allowing it to become purer and purer and purer. That is our wish. That is our hope. It will not happen in one day. It will take time for this all to transform. Your planet will be an awakened planet that has peace, love, harmony, joy, and caring in it for children and for all the ones who are here. That is what we are hoping to see here on this planet Earth ... love, respect, honoring, and abundance. For that, we will send information on how to grow food, we will send information, and higher-consciousness souls will be given to the Earth who will be seeded with all the things that your Earth will need and will be given. Food-wise and government-wise, everything will be balanced beautifully. We're hoping that you, who are reading this book, are listening to me and that we can open your heart with the new beginnings.

CHAPTER 10

Oceana, "The Night of Lights" (Public Talk, 12/30/1987)

Oceana, "The Night of Lights," Trance-Channeled by Amritam (December 30, 1987)

Amritam is a breath therapist and counselor. She has been channeling Oceana since April 1987. Oceana is a cluster of twenty-four nonphysical beings from a parallel universe. They have come to the Earth to help us in this timing. The Twenty-Four work as one unit and refer to themselves as *we*. Their message is *love*. Their main purposes for being here are to have a good time and to find people who are willing to study and look at new ways in working with children, teenagers, and the elders. Oceana has come to help us remember who we are. Some of the ways they are assisting us are through classes, weekend seminars, private sessions, and introductory open evenings. The following excerpts are taken from an introductory evening held on December 30, 1987, which Oceana called "The Night of Lights."

This evening is a time for you to look into your own light within, and it is a very beautiful night to set forth your new year with understanding of *who you are*. We are delighted to greet all of you on this wondrous night! We have called it "The Night of Lights," and that is what it is. Each of you—every night—*are the light*! This is something you have forgotten, and we have come to remind you. You have created the reflection, whether you know it or not. Isn't that exciting? You didn't know you were this wondrously powerful. And don't you think a *night of lights* is appropriate? It's like honoring yourselves. Children remember their light; they have not forgotten who they are. Wondrous is the part of you that *remembers* how beauteous you were as a child and how you have wonderment still within you. That means that, when you look into the evening stars, and you see them glittering in the *night of lights*, you realize that it is *you*! And it always has been, and you're in wonderment at the beauties that each of you are. You all know how to do everything. You all know that it's not really real! Not like the way you think it's real. It's like watching a movie. If you can step back from time and space long enough, then the attachment of the dramas you create in this life will lighten up. *There is no way to know what's true or not, unless you have a direct experience of it.* So enjoy yourselves as much as you can. And let your heart open up, and maybe you can have an experience of where you came from. Maybe you can look deep inside, and for one evening, drop all your mind's ideas of *who you are*, and *what is right*, and what is wrong in this world. And go back to that moment when you knew *who you were*. Meditation will take *all* of you and put you into your light, bring you to the point of *light*. Meditation does that, you know. It's not a new thing; it's very, very, very old and from the moment of beginning. For, without meditation and silence, and beyond what it takes you to, you could not be on the Earth. And without it, the *light* we talk about—*the night of lights*—will not be ignited again. And that's why you're all here! You want to ignite your *light*! That's why you do the work you do, that's why you fight when you fight, that's why you laugh when you laugh, that's why you make love when you make love with someone. That's why you make up good games, and play them, and find out how to get the right answers. *It's all about going home to that light that's in each of you!* We hope that something we say touches your heart. Someway, a part of you that has been closed gets opened again! So all we can ask of you is to let us in! And drop all your thinking, all your ideas of what is real and isn't real, and what we're doing here. *We're here because we love. That's it!* No interwoven thing is happening here, except *love.* We see beauty and love in each of you. *Love* is not making love with someone. Love is not soulmates. *Love* is a *moment of truth in your heart when you're ready to receive it. It's a sharing of time and space. It's available to all of you in this room tonight, and in every moment.* Look in your hearts, and see what you're holding on to. Some hurt or anger or even joy! Let it go and let it be! An empty space will appear within you, and the *light* will find you, and an abundance of joy can happen again! *Because, without joy, without wanting to be here totally, there is no way any of you can go home!* We want to talk about children and how important they are; how to nurture them in the most beauteous way that you can. Sometimes, when you become adults, you forget the children you were, and the love that's in you. You expect your children to know how one is, grown up. Instead of letting them play, and be in their world that is theirs, you want them to act like adults. Forget it! All of you adults think you are running this show and must teach them the right and wrongs of life. Instead, look at them as the masters; treat them like they are goddesses and gods, and protect them. That's your job! And let them experience the *love* in the world, and the flowers, and the trees, and the sand. And don't put your wishes upon them. *They're not yours!* Your child is all children; they are their own child, and you are here to guard them as they're growing upward. That's it! That's your only job. *Children teach you how to come home! Now we will tell you a story.* Now, as we talk, just close your eyes, and imagine that, as you sit here, *you're going to become lighter.* Take a very deep breath within yourself, and allow yourself to breathe all the way down to the base of your spine. And relax! Let go of all of your thoughts. Get comfortable—relax within your chair, or wherever you're sitting—and what's going to happen is, within your heart, you'll feel a sense of lightness coming upon you as we call the Twenty-Four into the room. From time past to now, to future, and time that was long forgotten ... A time when your universe was nothing but *light*! And very beauteous. In the center of the *light* was a golden color. On the outer part of the *light* was a white light, and around that was lavender. And that's what your universe looked like: *a beautiful light*, if you were to watch it. And in the center of that *light* is *all of you*! All of your aspects of *who you are*. All that you could ever imagine, with the most wondrous imagination you could ever have of *who you were*. In all of your *wonder*, and *knowledge*, and *truth*, and *clarity*, and *power, was one unity energy*. And then, one day, because the intelligence of this universe was so tremendously bright, you all wondered, "What would happen if we all split up into little *lights*, and searched out a place in the universe where we could live and communicate as individual *lights*, and become one unit anytime we want? What would happen if we did that?" So, slowly, slowly, you started separating —one by one. Flashes of lavender disappeared from the unit of love— the unit of *all*, the unit of *light*! And slowly, slowly, as time passed, this movement went on; segments of the original love separated. Slowly, slowly, you separated, until you knew all the knowledge was in each cell of *who you were*. Just imagine, that on your trip of *light*, you floated downward, or upward, to the planet of Earth—and a new game was created. You all did it together! You chose it consciously! You drifted onto the Earth, each of you as a *light*! *A god! A goddess, all that is, and all that shall be—ever!* You appeared on the Earth! With all your knowledge intact, in all your brightness. And, if you relax right now, and breathe, some of you can even tune in—or use your imagination in its most wondrous form—to how you looked when you entered the Earth, this Earth! For some, it could have been on another planet; for others, it's here. And just imagine how you looked in your royalty of God. And think of the knowledge you once knew. Now we're going to call that part of you, that's still in there, toward you. And breathe, and listen to the music, and relax ... and relax ... feeling your *light* above you, feeling your love around you. White around you, and lavender, and *love.* Calling in what you looked like in your enlightenment, when you knew *who you were.* Breathe ... breathe ... breathe ... deeper ... and deeper ... and deeper ... Calling the *light* to you. Calling, bringing it to you, as if you see some star as *you!* A mirror of your assets ... A mirror of your love. *Remembering who you are.* Letting go ... Let your knowledge come back to you ... Ask for it! Call it to you! It's your right, you know. It is your right—of each and every one of you—*to go home!* And look at yourself. Look at your *light*, your darkness, your joy, your truth, your shadows of darkness that are hidden, the parts of yourself you don't love, the fears, the anger you have at the world; that you had to come here, and you forgot who you were. *Look at all of it! And then remember.* Remember the love you once felt from the Divine, from the wondrous of all. *It's yours! Command it to you! And look!* For some of you, it will be a golden *light*, a glow; for some, a jewel; for some, a being; for some, an image of nothing. Whatever it is, look deep inside ... *It's there! You are the light! In this night of lights*, command it! Sit with it! Ask it to come to you. And breathe ... and breathe some more ... And, as the image appears to you, reach out with your hand, and ask for *truth* to be given ... Ask for *knowledge* to be given, and for help in the Earth plane. *A truth* ... let it come, bring it to you. And when you see this entity of the God that you are, *dance* with it! *Sing* with it! *Become it!* And *celebrate ... and celebrate ... and celebrate ... and celebrate ... and celebrate ... and celebrate ... That word is your way home!* And sometimes, there is fear in celebration. Dance with that too! And now, as this story goes, you chose to forget that you were God. You chose to forget, and now is the time that you can each *remember!* If you so choose, it means a lot ... celebrating each moment, and being a part of it. And fear? Well, it's got to leave. And the dark shadows; you've got to love them, accept them, and let them go. A dance wouldn't hurt any of you ... and, of course, you'd have to *remember you're responsible! And the creator of all! You can't blame anyone else ever again for the way your life is. You'll have to let it go, folks! But we guarantee, you'll become lighter! And life will change its course, and the dramas will disappear, the love will dance within your heart, and you'll become strong and powerful, and you will dance with every moment with the breath that has been given to you!* Why not? Why are you all holding on so tightly? Do you want to come *home?* You've got to get lighter ... and lighter ... and lighter ... physically, mentally, inwardly, outwardly ... *all parts of you! Nothing you're doing is real.* It's all a game! Why not become lighter with it? Why not be in the joys of it? Well, you might die; it's true. But not like you think! That old darkness will disappear, and you'll be *light!* And the shadows will be gone, and the fear will leave. *It's up to you!* And if you see your essence, well, good work! And if you don't, it's waiting for when you're ready. And some of you are going to sing it out into the world, some of you are going to draw, some of you are going to just listen to people talk, and some of you are going to run away and pretend it's not true. But that's up to you. *For you create your own reality any way you want!* You're in the driver's seat, and in the power. *We've told you how you came here, and we've told you how you can come home! It's up to you!* Each of you is always in your own choice and have the *truth within you. You also have the ability to change your reality at any moment, any way you want it.* You want to be a millionaire? Well, the only one stopping you is you! You want to have seven love affairs? Well, the only one stopping you is you! You want to dance all night? Well, the only one stopping you is you! You want to have three businesses? Well, the only one stopping you is you! *Take responsibility for it, and let it be! Love comes from within! You can't come home unless you lighten up! Enjoy yourselves now! Let go, and have fun doing it, and your dreams will all happen! Let go, and have fun doing it!* If you choose tonight, tomorrow, whenever, *that this is enough of this past misery, that this is enough of darkness and unconsciousness, and this is enough of wanting all these wants and not allowing yourself to have it—just say, so be it! It ends now! You do that, and your life will begin to transform! Just by the fact that you said, "So be it! It ends now!" Love yourself, and your dreams and others' dreams will begin to blossom. Your world is being forced into awareness! If you communicate the truth, it all happens!* That's the way it works. *That's what's up for your world right now. It's turning into godliness!* We're not going to create your reality for you. But we know you can do it well. *We came here to teach, and now we're going to do it! And we're going to speed things up!* It's not a lot of hard work here, folks; it's not! You're making it hard because you think you're not *doing* anything if it's not hard. You think you're not *growing!* Let me tell you; the *simpler* things are, the more *enlightened* they are. *Simplicity! Start taking your own life in hand, with light,* and remember to send your *light* out into the world. *You're beginning a new world and a new life! Dance with it! And have a good time! Know you're loved. Even if you don't feel it. Even if you're afraid of it. Even if you don't want us to love you. Just know it's true! You've always been loved. We love you. All of us, from all the universes. Peace, love, joy and light! Have a wondrous year!* .

—Oceana and the Twenty-Four

CHAPTER 11

Oceana's Selected Public Talks

Meditation and Forgiveness (September 17, 2015)

Alright, we are here, and good evening. We are Oceana and the Twenty-Four, and we are delighted that each of you have come. Each of you have been very sincere in your spiritual life and have been looking, studying, and meditating for some time. That's beautiful because it has helped each of you to raise your vibration and your consciousness of awareness. A lot of people don't really understand that meditation is very important for them. They don't understand that they are not just a body. They are a soul. Each of you in this room have a soul. I'm not so sure you are all connected to your souls, because you can't really see your souls. Your soul is in you. I've just been thinking about it. I've been on a couple of conferences in the universe here because we are all gathering together. We know that things can be handled beautifully if people are meditating, if people are in their hearts and helping each other and balancing their negativity. There is a very huge group of meditators and people who have been studying with many masters on this planet. There is also a huge group of people who don't understand all of that and don't even believe in it. When things start happening in your world, things will change and they will start coming to meditate. People who have not meditated, people who don't really understand ... it's not because they don't want to; it's just that they have not been turned on to it or they don't understand it. Each of you are important in that. You've been studying for thirty years from Osho and everybody, and you've been with Amritam and Oceana for twenty years or so, and many of you have studied with other masters. You are all beautiful people who have come to help humanity. You carry higher souls from all of your meditation and from being with enlightened masters. You people are very lucky. You have all met enlightened masters, right here in this building. I am one of them, Master Sha is one of them, Dattatreya Siva Baba, ... who else came here? Many different ones ... Prem Baba was here many times. Many enlightened ones have come here, and so you're going to see them traveling to remind people that this is a very important time in your world. You have been studying, going inside, and connecting with your soul and the light being you are. Connecting with why you came here and what you are doing to raise your vibration and bring it into more consciousness, awareness, and love. Everybody is needed for that. Everybody needs to go inside, meditate, and ask their souls what they can do to help humanity and help themselves become more conscious and more aware. We're trying to gather people so I can teach them certain meditations of protection, certain meditations of healing, and meditation for the soul to call their souls forward. I will do one tonight where I'll take you into meditation where you can, in a way, call your soul to you to give you information. Your soul is already there. You can't call it, but I'm saying call the information. Your soul is always within you, but I'm saying you can speak to your soul and get the answers you need. I will give a meditation tonight on that. I really want to continue to stress that this room needs to be filled with meditators, because when you all meditate, you help humanity. You stop the negativity that causes the imbalance on your Earth. Not just you, but when you all come together, you are powerful. You get five thousand people sitting here meditating, and Boulder's going to be the light place, let me tell you, if those kinds of things can happen. Boulder's a very special town because the Buddhist Trungpa Rinpoche came here. He was very, very beautiful, and he created a beautiful space of light here in Boulder so that the Buddhists who are here are still meditating and still doing that work, and it keeps Boulder balanced. All of you who may not have been with Trungpa, if you meditate and go deep inside, you are also helping humanity. One thing that has to happen, if you don't have yourself together, you have to help yourself first, and then you can help others. You need to get your life together so that you are balanced mentally, physically, and emotionally and that takes time. Everybody should help each other get balanced. The more you work together, the more powerful Boulder will be in the transition to help others move through things. Boulder is a pretty good place to live. You're not by the ocean, you are not by the volcanoes; you're in a good spot, although things can still happen. Mountains can be difficult, but I don't see any eruptions. There are some mountains farther away from here, but at this point, I don't see volcanoes happening here. I do see a lot happening in your oceans from underneath. They don't even know about it. It's not so much the nature; it's the things you have built, like nuclear bombs and radiation and things like that. Things like the ones leaking in Japan. All that is part of the transition. In time, it's very difficult because you have so many different cultures and so many ideas and so many brains that have forgotten the Source, and they have forgotten they are even on this planet. They would not even have anything they have in their lives if it weren't for the Divine, the beauty, and the love. You will see in time … it won't happen overnight, but slowly, people will awaken again.

It will be a grand university in heaven. We'll call it the university of heaven. I like that very much; they gave me that … the grand university in heaven. It's grand because people will be in delight. People will be in love; people will be in caring. People will share their intelligence, their beauty, their hearts, and they will take responsibility, which is responding in the here and now with love for themselves and then others. You have to find your way of awakening, your way of taking responsibility for your life and helping others. If you haven't helped yourself, you can't really help others, so you have to work very diligently on meditation. Find your niche of what you love to do, and do it. Find your way on the Earth that works for you. Take responsibility, and don't just be here with no higher longing. Like everyone in this room, just for a minute, close your eyes. What have you wanted to do in your life that would help you and humanity? You may not know yet, but it's a question. When you are helping yourself, when you are becoming strong again and using the talents that the Divine has given you, then you can help humanity. You can't do that until you get strong in yourself. Many people have suffered here, and many people have had tragedy. Many people haven't been able to do that because the hurt and pain in their lives were too grand, and it's taken time for them to heal. That's all beautiful, and you just keep healing. The Divine is a whole karmic thing, but you can heal. You can forgive; and truly, truly, forgiveness will be the only way for this planet to survive. Forgiveness, forgiveness to anyone who has ever hurt you and forgive yourself for who you have hurt. It's great to forgive someone else, but if you're not forgiving yourself, it's no good, even though they forgave you. You're still beating yourself up. That won't work. You have to move to forgiveness. Everybody who comes to this Earth makes mistakes, some horrible mistakes. It's all part of the transformation. It's all part of karma. Good karma, in-between karma, and supreme karma, and really having to go inside and move to forgiveness. I can't stress it enough. I've been speaking about it for years now, and I watch the people. Some people are so filled with hurt and anger that they can't forgive. Some people are so forgiving that they don't take care of themselves, and then they hurt themselves, thinking that they are not good or something. Forgiveness is so important. You must forgive those who have hurt you. You must forgive yourself for hurting yourself by not taking responsibility for your life ... forgiveness, forgiveness, forgiveness. I'm not saying it's easy; I am not saying that to you. I'm saying it's the key to your world. It's the key that has to happen. I don't know if it can, because there are so many different cultures, so many different countries, and so many imbalances on the Earth. There are so many people who have to go through certain things, especially in warring countries. We're hoping that the more the masters come, the more we stress forgiveness on the planet, the more your country will not be in as much trauma as things change. If forgiveness happens, it won't be as bad. When forgiveness happens, even the Earth forgives. The ocean forgives; the streams forgive; the light forgives; the stars forgive; the energy of the Earth is in peace, love, and balance. I know it is not easy. I know people have been hurt, I know you've hurt people so you can't forgive yourself either; but forgiveness is the answer. Forgiveness is the answer. That is the way home for this planet and each person in this room and in this world. I will be doing a lot more speaking to teach people about forgiveness and to teach people meditations that can balance themselves and their Earth so that things don't have to be so traumatic. I'll also be teaching you about forgiving yourself. That's the first place you have to start, by forgiving yourself before you can forgive anybody else. The Earth is not an enlightened planet. This is for people who come here to receive, to grow, to awaken, to forgive, to transform; and maybe there is some enlightenment in there, depending on the Divine and how many enlightened ones the Divine has sent to your planet to help raise the vibration here. These are enlightened ones that have already reached enlightenment and have come to your Earth to help those who are in the process of awakening. I am going to be helping people to do these forgiveness practices. Meditation is number one for the transition. Number what? One! When you meditate, you go deeply into your soul, and you get connected with the Absolute, where you all come from. When you can connect with the Absolute, transformation can happen instantly. Those of you who've been studying, those of you who understand the Divine, who understand meditation, who have been meditating, who have experienced that you are light, those of you who continue to do your meditations … continue to come to a place like this, or wherever you are comfortable. I'm not saying everybody has to come to this temple. I'm saying you go where you want to go … but go. And this temple is very protected. This calligraphy (Oceana points to the calligraphy drawn by Master Sha) shows that we are oneness. So we have brought many masters. There's not just one master. We are a temple of oneness. I will be gathering people in oneness; and masters in oneness will be coming together, which has never happened. It's going to take a huge amount of enlightened ones to help each other. It's like somebody lights a candle, and you light another one, and another one, and another one, and another one, and each light carries its light. Everybody carries consciousness, everybody carries beauty, everybody carries love, everybody carries anger, hurt, and pain. You have to forgive and forget it. Know that, whatever happened to any of you, it was karma. You forgive yourself, you forgive the karma, and you move forward. Don't dwell on it. It's a waste of time. Just start new every day, every day, every day … and take responsibility for your own negativity, and lift yourself up through meditation and love. If any of you need help, you go to the doctor and you get help in balancing your mental abilities if they are off. You balance mental, physical, and emotional bodies by meditating and being with me and other masters. So that is basically what I am telling you. You are a very small group, but you can go tell your other people, "Come on. Oceana is going to get you to open your heart, meditate, and forgive. If you don't forgive, you are stuck, and they are stuck." The more people who move to forgiveness, the more people who love, the more people who care, the more your Earth will not be so affected. Just know that everybody is a little unbalanced on your Earth because you're not enlightened. If you have a couple tantrums or something today, just put yourself back into meditation and forgive yourself and the Earth (or whatever or whomever you were disturbed by) and let it go, people. Let it go, like your parents and people who weren't right. Just let it go. It's only hurting you. Be in the here and now. That's where you have to be. When you do that, aren't you happier? When you are in the here and now, you get to look at the stars. It's so beautiful, it's so wonderful, when you sit in meditation and you feel the ancient one in you, you feel the beauty in you, and your heart begins to open. I will take you into meditation. So get yourself in a comfortable position. I will be giving a lot more meditations. I will be doing a new schedule for this beautiful place Amritam found. She has kept it this long, and it's not easy. Not everybody understands meditation, but it's God's will to have this place continue. It's a beautiful retreat center of love and light. The energies and the saints that come here … you have no idea. This is their home as well, and they love all of you. One day, you'll see quite a few people coming because they will need help. Most people have forgotten meditation, but we will help them. We will put meditations out, and we will put books out; and when they come in through the gate, all negativity cannot come in. So remember that for your own healing. This is a beautiful space of meditation because this is a vortex of light.

Meditation/Visualization: The Calling and Forgiveness (September 24, 2015)

Alright, so just close your eyes. Take three deep breaths. Take another deep breath with your mouth open. Let go of my talk and go inside to your heart. Dearest ones, this is Oceana. I am from the ocean. "Cean" is the wind, and "ana" is the female aspect of the Divine. We have come to your Earth to bring love, peace, joy, harmony, and a new way to raise this beautiful planet into love. Love that is eternal. Love that heals all wounds; love that touches the heart, the mind, the being, the ancient one that's within you. We have come to call forth all the ancient, enlightened ones. We call forth all of your higher selves, all of the souls that are in the process of moving to enlightenment. We are calling you home to the light. We are calling you to the ancient ones. We are calling you to let go of your past. We are calling you to ask the Absolute to come to you, to help you awaken, to help you forgive, to help you give to those who need love, caring, joy, and abundance of love for all of humanity. For those who have forgotten, we are sending all the ancient ones to come and fill you with love, fill you with forgiveness, and fill you with the Divine. For each of you carry a spark of the Divine. When you begin to believe, when you begin to call forth God, the Absolute, and all there is, the spark ignites in your heart. When that happens, you are on a new journey, a journey of God finding the ancient God within you that has been dormant for so long. The spark gets lit, and your heart opens. You relax, you trust, you believe, you care for the oceans and the trees, the forest, the sky, the atmosphere, the light, the sun, the moon, the mountains, and the rivers. You all open your hearts, and new ways to heal your Earth will be given. For the Divine, the Absolute, all there is and all there shall ever be is holding you in the arms of the Absolute. Rocking you like a child, bringing you home to forgiveness, bringing you home to creation, bringing you home to creativity, bringing you home with knowledge to heal your rivers, your oceans, and your mountains. The mountains can erupt. When they feel the meditation, when they experience the Earth coming back into balance, they will never erupt. Peace will be here, love will be here, abundance will be here, kindness will be here, and joy will be here. Those who are imbalanced and need help will be taught; they will be uplifted, they will be forgiven, and they will be given knowledge; and then they can help in balancing the universes with love, with peace, with forgiveness. I, Oceana, have come to call you all home. To bring you to meditation, so you can take these meditations and do them at home. So you can share them with your families, your children, and your friends and let them know there is help coming. Through meditation, through the space of forgiveness, bring them here. Sit in the bliss and the light of all the saints that come. Feel your soul, and you say, "Dear soul of mine, thank you for helping me in all these lives. Thank you for sending me to enlightened ones. Thank you for giving me a chance to forgive. Thank you for uplifting this Earth so we can all come back to oneness and the beauty of God which each of you carry." The seed of God will be ignited, and you will rise slowly, slowly in time, when it's appropriate, to enlightenment. We love you, and we honor you all who are here. We honor all the enlightened masters who are on this planet holding it together. We honor all the saints, all the awakened ones, all the levels of consciousness, all the dimensions beyond this Earth who are sending love, light, beauty, kindness, and peace. Take a deep breath, and thank God in your own way. Thank all the ancient ones, thank your higher self, thank the Earth, the rivers, the oceans, and the mountains. Thank them for being here. Thank yourself for finding meditation. Forgive all those who've hurt you, and forgive yourself if you've ever hurt anyone. It's all part of transformation to light, to peace, to harmony, to joy, and to purity. Send light to all the children. All the young ones. Send light to the rivers, the oceans, the mountains, and all the enlightened masters that are on the planet. Thank them, and thank yourself for being a meditator. Thank you, if you are bringing people to come and find this knowledge; bring them, bring them. What will happen when things start happening? They will come running. Just look them in their eyes and say, "Don't worry, God's with you. Don't worry, God's with you. Don't worry, God's with you. We are all with you. For there is no death. Maybe of the body, but not of your soul. You're immortal, eternal, and you'll continue to rise with love, love, and more love; and joy, joy, and more joy." Everybody, take a deep breath. Oh, take another one; it feels so good, it feels so good. Thank your soul for bringing you tonight. Thank the calligraphy which is sending light to all of you. Thank Oceana and the Twenty-Four. We love you, we honor you, we forgive you, and we ask you to forgive us. Forgiveness is the key. Don't forget it. Thank you for coming to this beautiful night. I will end it. Then come again, and bring your friends; they need to know so we can help them.

Meditation/Visualization: Connecting with the Soul for Service to Humanity (from Oceana's Public Talk, September 24, 2015)

Alright, well, we are here, and good evening! We are delighted to meet you all here again tonight ... seeing you coming back on this beautiful night. I liked what Amritam said that we'll be doing during this meditation tonight, and they'll make more of that CD so you can get them to take home. So, each night that you come, I'll be doing different kinds of meditations, bringing mental, physical, and emotional balance and helping you be more aware of your body and your soul. So, for the first thing before I do the meditation, I would like everybody to just close your eyes and just listen to what I say. So you say inside, "Dear soul, mind, and body, I love you. Dear soul of mine, I love you. Dear soul within me, I am ready to experience the power, the love, the beauty of my soul. I am now ready to thank you for guiding me in this life. Thank you for the gifts and ideas you have given me that have uplifted me, my family, my friends, and my work. Dear soul, I am hoping to connect with you more often. Dear soul, the ancient one that I am. I am going to meditate more so that I can carry the balance of mental, physical, and emotional bodies." As you are sitting there now with your eyes closed, sitting up straight and comfortable, you say inside—just repeat not out loud, but inside—"Dear soul of mine, I am in deep gratitude. I am here on this Earth, in this bodily form, and you are within me; the soul that is wise, that is ancient, that is love, that is creative, and that has helped me so often in this life. I'm asking in my heart to connect more in my soul to get to know the ancient one within me. So I will close my eyes, like I am now, and I want to thank you for your love, for your consciousness, for your wisdom, for your protection, and for this beautiful body that you are within. Thank you for your guidance, thank you for your love, thank you for guiding me to the right directions of the Divine, thank you for leading me into a life that is conscious, aware, forgiving, giving, and receiving to those around me. I am so grateful, dear soul of mine." So now, as you are sitting, just inside, speak to your soul. Ask a question, or ask them to give you advice. Say, "Dear soul of mine, give me an answer to this question, or give me advice from within." Remember to tell them you love them. This is just a way tonight to get you in using your soul and actually really going into meditation and connecting with the ancient one in you that can give you comfort, ideas, knowledge, and ways to raise your consciousness, your awareness of who you are, what you are doing here, and what your dreams and hopes are. How are you going to give your love to not only yourself but to others? And how are you going to share your life with friends and other people? Really go in, and realize it, and ask a very important question like, what is it that your soul came here to do and finish? Before you can do that, you have to open up the doorway for communication. We will work with the soul, and we will work with other things that you have questions about in your life and about how to raise your consciousness and your meditation skills. By being consistent, you'll be surprised how much shifts in your life. Think, "I'm going to raise my consciousness. I'm going to connect with my soul. What is it that I'm longing for? What am I longing for? What am I looking for? What is it?" I don't mean just in the everyday life, and I mean the everyday life. What is it that you are doing here, and how do you want to continue to raise your consciousness and life? What do you want to do in service for humanity? There's nothing greater than serving humanity. It's what you have come here to do, to support, if you have ways of doing that. Just like people come and set up the room, they are supporting your coming tonight. There are people recording; they are supporting, growing. There are events we have that people are getting to connect with. There will be more and more people coming, because as things transform, people are going to need more help. So all the meditation you've done, all the work you've done with people, will all come to fruition. What is it that you are really wanting to empower yourself with through meditation and consciousness? What do you want to do now in your life? This is not to say to stop doing what you are doing, but is there anything now that is a new idea? One of the best ways to raise your consciousness is to celebrate your life, and I'm not so sure you are all doing that. I see worry in things, I see kind of clocking out, I see guilt and shame still happening, disappointment still happening, or anger still. All that's got to go, and that takes time. So how you heal that is by looking at it and forgiving it. Forgive yourself and others. If you can do that, you'll rise right away. That takes courage and really going in and meditating and saying, "OK, I need to forgive this, and that, and this, and that. I have to really look. How do I want my life to be now? How am I going to support myself and others? How am I going to be in service to humanity in a way that will bring me happiness and others happiness?" Because what else are you going to do here? Otherwise, you'll waste a whole life and have to do it again. You've got to have some fun here with it all and enjoy it and be here. That is why Amritam tries to get people to move, because if people move (even if they're just sitting in the chair), they can move right so things start moving. When you start moving, things start moving. That's why we try to do the dancing with people, because what happens is that you unlock your brain. The endorphins go into your brain, and you can think better. You can come up with better ideas and do all those things. One thing you do know is that laughter is the cure. You've got to laugh at yourself. You've got to laugh about what you get mad about. You've got to laugh about what you are happy about. You've got to forgive yourself, you've got to forgive all the goofy people in your life, and just let it go. Let it go because it stops you. It stops your life from flowering. You want it to flower. Sit down and really look at what you want and how you want your life to be. So you want to look for your love affair with something creative for you, whatever it is. Writing, dreaming, taking pictures ... it doesn't matter. Whatever turns you on, it should be bringing you happiness. It shouldn't be a problem. It should be bringing your joy to you, not suffering. So that's what I'm saying to all of you. Just so you know, there is a lot going to be happening. All of you are going to need to help your friends and people, and really look inside and get your consciousness, meditate, speak to your souls, get yourselves on track, and do things you love. If you are doing what you love, there might be something you've left out, so you might want to think about whether there is anything you have forgotten about. People who laugh live longer. People who play live longer. People who move live longer. People who help each other live longer. They've already got proof on that. You might meditate more, and as you meditate, you become looser. What do I mean by that? Lighter … lighter is the better word, but looser. These people have been coming to me for a long time, and they have done everything. They've cried, they've laughed, they have just done anything, and they have gotten everything straightened out. They forgave themselves and others, and that's what happens when you let go and you realize that this is your life. You don't want to waste it and have to do it all again. You want to live with your heart open. You want to serve not only yourself, but other people; because when you serve other people, you change your life. Now you can't always serve people until you get yourself balanced. You've got to get yourself balanced first, then you can go for it. So these people have been around a long time, and they are still listening to me. You know why? Because they get higher and higher and higher, and what they are higher in is love, compassion, and forgiveness. All those things you used to walk in here with are gone, all the suffering and problems and all that. You just forgave, and now you are free. You get to be free. That's cool. Is that a good word? Yes … that's a good word. I have to check every once in a while if I am speaking properly. We have five acres of land here. We can gather many people here to meditate and keep your Earth balanced. When you all move into meditation, imagine five hundred people all in the hum! It changes this Earth, so I send a blessing to you. Have a beautiful evening! I love you all, and I know your souls. I don't know your personalities, but I know your souls.

This is a calligraphy. This one is from China. (Pointing to Master Sha's picture.) He's enlightened. He did this calligraphy. When you trace it, it heals people; it heals your heart, your soul, and who you are. This calligraphy has been given from this ancient master. His name is Master Sha now, but he's an old one. There are more old ones from all over Europe. All over everywhere, they will slowly come together with ancient knowledge and ancient ways to heal. Nobody believes it, but there are things happening on your Earth. Amritam gives blessings to people every day with this calligraphy. Thank you all for coming. We send love and joy. OK, we are going to close the night now.

Oceana "Align with the Divine Course talk" (October 22, 2015)

Alright, well, we are here, and good evening! We are delighted to attend this evening's first event. Everybody wants to live life beautifully. Everybody wants to be connected to God. Everybody wants to be in alignment with the Divine, whether they talk about it or not. Whether they are afraid is another question, because they have forgotten they are human beings. They have forgotten they each carry a soul. They have forgotten they are in a process each lifetime of uplifting their souls. So I'm not just talking to your body or your mind or your mental concepts or your childhood, good or bad or whatever it was. I'm talking to your ancient soul that doesn't think like your mind. So I'm not talking to that part of you. I'm talking to your soul, and your soul is ancient. Your soul knows what to do. Your soul has to be nourished and fed because you have neglected it. Not because you wanted to, but because your world has forgotten that every human being is made from the Divine. You have a cell. Every single human being has a cell of the original Divine's presence that was given to the Earth. Do I mean that you carry the cell of the Divine? Yes. Does everybody? Yes. What does that mean? That means, when it's time and you are called, you will come back to the original god self you are. That's why you have come to the Earth. Nobody has ever told that secret but me. It means you carry a cell from the Divine's presence; but if you don't know it, you can't contact it. One cell from God is all you need! It means you've got to think big. Nobody told that secret. You know why? Because they weren't allowed. It's alright now because we have to call the people, and the people are listening. They need to learn meditation. They need to learn what Jesus knew, what God knew. They need to learn to hold the winds away. They need to learn to stop the oceans from drying up. They need to learn how to love the children; to empower them; to give them knowledge, peace, and harmony; to be cared for. God has much compassion and loves all beings, no matter what they've done or haven't done. All of you have gone through restructuring, whether you remember it or not. That's why you are in this meditation class (or any other meditation class, or you're with any other masters you sorted out). This information is very, very important. They are going to teach you meditation. They are going to teach you how to go inside, to your heart. You are going to find the soul that you are and the ancient one that you are. You are going to be able to help not only yourself, but also others in the transition by being uplifted through meditation. "Align with the Divine." What are we aligning with? What's the Divine? You carry the seed of all there is. In this course, you are going to go inside, you are going to meditate, you are going to find the presence of your higher self or your soul or whatever you want to call it.

The inner peace of God that you carry. If you are serious, if you are connected, and if you believe in your meditations, in different moments in time, you will have a connection with God or all there is. Even though some of you already have that, this will be more. This will be what you've been waiting for. So everybody, just close your eyes. Please sit up so your spine is erect, as best you can. See, that way it gives no bumps. I don't know what to call it. Twists and turns. You know God loves laughter. God loves people. God laughs with people. God plays with people. God enjoys life and embraces life. When God eats a piece of fruit, it's like magic. When God dances, it is like the most beautiful moment in time. When God makes love to the world, it's like nothing you could ever imagine. You are so loved. You are so cared for. The Divine tries very hard to uplift all the souls and wants all of you to be uplifted. We will keep calling them and calling them, and they will find us. Those who are true will be uplifted into higher consciousness and higher states of love. Whether you leave your body or not, you are taken to the highest consciousness. If your heart is open, if your heart loves, if the heart forgives people ... it's very important ... forgiveness for all your lives where you've hurt people or they've hurt you. When you really forgive, your doorways open to God. None of you are perfect. All of you have made mistakes, every human being on the planet. So, if you can forgive yourself, your parents, your relatives, and goofy people out there—whoever they are—just forgive them. For they know not what they do. So you can't be mad at someone who doesn't know, who has no brain, no consciousness, and no awareness. You just send a blessing and ask God to help them because they need it. You see, that's love, that's heart, that's beauty. So, as you close your eyes, take a couple of deep breaths.

Meditation/Visualization: Connecting with Your Soul

OK, everyone, close your eyes. I'm calling all the Divine Beings here, all the saints, all the beautiful gifts and beings that have been coming to the temple to bless all those who walk here. We activate the calligraphy. We activate all the saints that are here. Please send your love to each one of these beautiful people who've come with open hearts, who've come with love. Take a nice, deep breath. Just go inside. Breathe deeply. Relax your body. Feel your feet on the ground. Then you say, "Dear soul of mine, I love you. I honor you. I am so grateful that you chose to be my soul. I am so grateful that I have found meditation. I have found the soul within, the Divine within me. And I'm beginning to remember the love that is in every cell of my body. I am beginning to remember that I am born of God, of the ancient one; that I carry the cells of the Divine, the love of the Divine, the magic of the Divine, and the beauty of the Divine. I am in great gratitude to life, to the Earth, to the sun, to the moon, and to the ancient ones that hold the Earth in balance. I am very grateful, and I am very lucky to be with you. I love you." Each of your souls love you. What I just said to you, I spoke from your beloved soul, telling you they love you, they are with you, they are here to watch you transform and uplift your heart and soul to God to be in service of humanity for yourself, for the people, for the Earth, and for the atmosphere. Each of you allow yourself to love the Earth and to love God. Now you say, "Dear soul of mine, awaken within my heart." They have to come. "Dear soul of mine, awaken within me." Now, as you go inside, say a prayer to them from your heart, and you can ask a question if you want. They will speak to you. If you are finished, just sit with your soul. OK, this exercise is extremely important. Slowly open your eyes. You need to meet your soul; not your brain, not your ideas, not your body, but your soul. Your soul has been trying to talk to you. You have to listen. They've loved you since you were a little boy or girl, and they have been knocking on you. But see what happened because they knocked on you? You got here. Your soul loves you so much. You have a big heart, and each of you care for human beings and the world. You all care, and you don't know what to do with your caring. That's why you've come here, because you are serious; you are ancient. You don't even believe that, but you can do good work just by your meditations. First, you meditate with your soul; and then, the soul in you sends the light to the people, your family, and the world. Sometimes, families don't get it. I understand that. When things start happening, and you are beaming, you are speaking to your soul, you are loving; and you look at one of them and say, "Let me help you. I'll teach you meditation. It will keep you balanced, and things will go easier for you because you'll be connected to God." The best way to help is to share your experience. When you sit in your meditations and your soul is speaking to you, jot some of the information down. They will give you help in your meditation, in your gardens, in your work, or in making money ... things like that. You will start being stronger in your soul and your body, meaning you will be in your state of love, of your heart. You want to be in your state of knowledge so you can be at the right places at the right times, and in the right meditations. People will ask, "Why are you glowing?" And you'll reply, "I meditate. I sit with my soul. I send love to the Divine and to the Earth and to humanity. And I thank God every day for the gifts that I've been given." You do that every day, and people will ask, "What happened? He's glowing. Oh, what happened? You are shining. What happened? He's not so grumpy anymore." And you will say, "Well, I've learned to meditate. My life is going really good, and I'm helping a lot of people. And you know what? I'm having a good time here." What are you doing? You can talk to God. You are that. You carry it. The Divine cannot not come, if you truly ask from the heart. It can't come for a test, like you'll ask God and see if He shows up! If your heart is in it, you will get an answer from the Absolute. Even the worst of worst will get an answer from God. Because God never has a no. He is always there to help, even if you have been really naughty. You are very innocent people. Each of your souls are ancient. It's very special. It's a gift. Your soul came into your body so you can uplift even higher, and your soul can uplift higher because it loves. From meditating, you look healthy, you feel better, you are happier, and you are not afraid anymore. You are strong, and you walk with God in you. You have certainty in your body, heart, and soul. You are not jealous, sad, or feeling that you didn't get this or that. You feel the presence of who you are and who your soul is. When you feel that, your soul kind of flowers and your life starts changing. I don't mean massive changes instantly; this little thing is different, like, "I don't feel that way anymore, I'm feeling a little healthier." Or, "I realize I'm a beautiful person." Or, "Oh, I know I can draw a beautiful picture. Oh I know I can walk with strength in my body and heart and soul. Or, "I'm not afraid anymore. I can be the man I am, with the knowledge I carry around." This is a very special course. You won't even recognize yourselves when it's finished. You'll realize that you've been given a gift that you've been waiting lifetimes for. And that gift is to recognize your soul. To know who you are. You might get an epiphany or an idea, or you might open your heart a certain way or get an "aha" moment. So you close your eyes, and go in, and ask your soul to give you a message of something that might happen or be given to you. They are going to give you a message for your upliftment of consciousness. Your soul is powerful, and it can help you in your everyday life, in your body, in your heart, in your mind, and in really going inside and connecting with the love you have for your soul and for humanity. Forgiveness is a big part of this. The things that keep people from having fuller lives is that they haven't forgiven. So there are many things ... sometimes, you just have to say, "I forgive all those lives because I can't remember them." If there are things in this life that you need to go in and forgive—and you just keep doing it—eventually, it goes away. Forgive yourself also, because everyone has made mistakes. That's usually the hardest part, to forgive yourself. You realize how much your soul has energy, knowledge, love, and information for each of you in your life—your work life, your home life, your love life, and your family life. All of that is what your soul is here to help you with, and to help with other things that you are working on for yourself. So, each of you, pick something that you want to uplift and transform or be more aware of. It could be that you want to write a book, or maybe you want to be healthier, or maybe you want to eat differently, or maybe you want to take a walk every day ... whatever it is you want to do for you. Maybe you want to write a poem every day ... something that you do for you. It could be mental, physical, or emotional, but you give yourself a gift every day. I'm asking about whatever you want to give yourself in your life or want to do something new. Something you want to do for yourself. Maybe you want to change your job. Maybe you want to meditate more. Maybe you want to get more serious about your spiritual life. Whatever is helping you in the uplifting of your consciousness. One of the things I do feel is that everybody should meditate and take good care of their bodies. Take good care of your body and get healthier, whatever that means to you. It's different for different people. Why do you want to do that? Because you will live longer, and it's a way to love yourself. When you love yourself, love just comes from you everywhere you go. It's not all about me, me, me, me, me ... I need, need, need, need, need ... me, me, me, me ... poor me, poor me, poor me, poor me. It's not about that. You are that love. You are beautiful.

You are the light. All of you want to be more in your hearts, want to be more conscious, want to be more loving, want to care, and want to help humanity. But you can't help humanity if you aren't helping yourself. So what I see is that some of you don't actually love yourselves. You kind of beat yourselves up. And so you don't allow that anymore. Because you are all beautiful. You don't let your mind be that mommy-and-daddy thing. You just love yourself. You make a mistake, and you say, "That's OK. We'll fix this. I'm all right, and I'm here on the planet. I love meditating. I love connecting with the Divine. I love learning, growing, and uplifting my soul and my life." These are the kinds of things I want you to think about in your life. Just think, if you are thinking positively every day— instead of negatively— what kind of transformation you are going to create in your life. It's not going to go away instantly. A lot of you have really bad patterns. So you just don't allow it. You say, "Oh, there it is again." Turn it around, and make it positive. "Oh there it is again," and you just laugh. "My brain is such a silly brain." You just watch it. So just close your eyes. I'll give a little meditation. Everybody, take a nice deep breath. Relax, and you say inside, "Dear soul of mine, I love you. Dear soul of my life, I love you. Dear all the beings I have ever hurt, please forgive me. Dear souls that have hurt me, I forgive you. Dear the wind, the trees, and the stars; the moon, the rain, and the food I eat; the animals, and the cars I drive, I love you. Thank you for all your service. Dear soul of mine, I love you. Thank you for keeping me safe, giving me ideas, teaching me, loving me, and supporting me in my life. Dear all the things I've ever received, thank you. Dear souls of anyone I've ever hurt, please forgive me. Dear all there is and all there shall ever be, I care about you. Thank you for this beautiful life I've been given. Thank you for all the lessons I've learned. Thank you for this new beginning so that I can be more conscious and aware and help myself and humanity. Thank you, thank you, thank you. I am in deep gratitude. Thank you, Divine. Thank you, God. Thank you, angels. Thank you, saints. Thank you, all the Divine Beings that are in this center. Thank you, thank you, thank you. Please help me to become more aware, more conscious, more healthy, and more awakened. Please allow me to raise my vibration, my heart, and my love to a high state of consciousness; to help not only myself and family, but humanity. Please, please, dear God, know that I am here as a servant to you and all there is. Thank you, thank you, thank you." Everybody, take a deep breath. We'll end the evening. Alright, have a great night.

Oceana's Talk: Align with the Divine Course
(October 5, 2015; Class Already in Progress)

Whatever it's saying, you know that if it's not positive, you are on the wrong rung right now. Somewhere, you've lost your consciousness, your heart, your love, and your understanding. You are here to learn; and sometimes, all the lessons are not always fun. So you have to watch your mind. You are here to come and grow. Become more aware, become more conscious. The brain has rungs on it, like this. And you grow up with having to watch your mother or father, sisters or brothers, and you have a lot of things filling your head. Anybody notice that? So, when you go into meditation, you end up being what we call the watcher, and you are no longer run by your mind, by your chitter-chatter, or by the way you were raised by your parents and all that. When you go into meditation, you find your soul again. And your soul doesn't get lost in that kind of stuff. It doesn't make people wrong. It doesn't allow you to be angry or hurt all the time, or throw tantrums, or be mad at the world, or make yourself bigger or better than anyone else, or be in competition with everybody … all those things you have to watch because they are not real. The only thing that's real is now, and you go inside, and you say, "Dear soul mind, body of my soul …" I'll say it again. "Dear soul mind, body of my soul, I love you. I honor you. I honor all beings of light, as appropriate. I am watching. I am now going inside to the beautiful presence that I am … it's very important." So close your eyes and sit up straight. Please sit up straight, because the energy in the spine rises when you meditate; and the other thing that is important when you finally find your interest and when you find what you call your spiritual journey is that there are things that you have to take care of. One is your body, because without the body, you can't be here. So you have to begin to be healthier, and meditation will help you to do that. Also, you want to be more aware of what you say, what you do, and who you are. So you begin to learn, "Oh, I am Satya." (A student in the room.) "I am watching Satya. Is this Satya the soul of mine, or is it my training as a child?" So what I'm saying is, when you become the watcher, you are aware of consciousness and also aware of higher consciousness, versus listening to how your mother complained all day; and suddenly, you are walking around complaining. Anybody ever have that happen? That you have a flashback, and it puts negativity in your head—negativity about other people, negativity about yourself, negativity. When that happens, it's very important for you to not allow it. Thank you very much. I am uninterested, mind, in your negativity, and then you look around where you are and say, "Oh my God. I live in a place where there are no wars. I live in a place where there's love. I live in a place where people care about each other. I am in a place where I have beautiful friends. I live in a town called Boulder that's supreme. I'm not in countries where people are dying. I'm not suffering like so many in the world. I am deeply grateful to the Divine, to my soul, and to God." So meditation can help bring you into a higher state of consciousness and positive thinking.

CHAPTER 12

Testimonials by Oceana and Amritam's Students

Testimonial by Ma Deva Geha (8/20/2017)

"Being in the presence of Oceana and the Twenty-Four empties my mind of all thought. Only pure love and light fills my heart and soul. Even after thirty years of being in their presence, this feeling still remains, and I rise ever upward in consciousness. I know I have come home; home to the love, purity, beauty, light, truthfulness, and glory of life everlasting. Listening to Oceana speak spiritual truths, one knows they are in the presence of enlightened beings. Oceana shares their love and beauty and makes your heart sing, knowing you have finally found love, joy, peace, and happiness within yourself. Oceana helps one clean their mirror of life to become their true self. Thank you, Oceana, for choosing Amritam, a pure channel, to bestow your love and knowledge to all souls on Earth. I am forever grateful to you, Oceana and the Twenty-Four. Forever your friend, Ma Deva Geha."

Testimonial by Melinda Laine

"I *love, love, love* Oceana and the Twenty-Four. I was first introduced to them by one of their beautiful meditations on Facebook online ... a message so simple and so impactful ... they said, 'Just close your eyes, and call to the Divine and to your soul ... and know that they are with you and around you at all times, and that we can ask the Divine to remove all obstacles in our way to have a more beautiful life.' I started this type of dialogue and experienced a noticeable upliftment of peace and joy, and I decided to join a workshop on opening your heart to love and light and balance. My hope at this point was to lose my 'edge.' We've gone way beyond that now. I haven't been able to work since 1999 due to severe clinical depression, PTSD, and two collapsed discs that have left me with limited feeling from the waist down (except for chronic back pain). Since participating in three Oceana workshops and following the suggestions, I am off *all* my pharmaceutical medications (something I have been trying to do for years with limited success). At the beginning of this process I would call on the Divine thirty or so times a day to get relief from emotional and physical pain. Now, two or three times a day is all that is required. As a little child, I walked the path of love, and I remember a beautiful relationship with God/Jesus, and then life happened and my heart closed. Oceana and the Twenty-Four gave me a key to a door I had locked a long, long time ago. I find their message simple to understand and easy to implement. Love, light, and balance. Finally, I want to share the best gift of all ... in a guided meditation with Oceana and the Twenty-Four, I felt the love of the Divine in a way that I could not question, and I will never doubt the love that the Divine or my soul has for me ever again ... I am free!"

Testimonial by Alan Whitman

"Amritam and Oceana and the Twenty-Four are powerful, wonderful, spiritual masters and teachers who have helped me and many, many people heal our hearts and uplift our consciousness. They are totally dedicated to love, oneness, compassion, service, and the upliftment of consciousness for humanity. They are here to help us connect with our souls, to remember who we really are and why we came to Earth, and to help humanity through Earth's transition. Amritam trance-channels Oceana, who is the speaker for the Twenty-Four, a group of enlightened beings that help guard the Earth. Their consistent love, deep caring, and understanding led to transformative spiritual experiences I had that are truly out of this world. I met Amritam and Oceana and the Twenty-Four in Boulder, Colorado, in 1988. My first private session with Oceana was like talking to an old friend who knew me as well as I knew myself. They knew things about me that only I knew. That session turned out to be the birth of my spiritual path. The first public talk of Oceana's that I went to was a year and a half after that first private session with them. There was a big crowd there ... about two hundred people in attendance. I was very touched by the reactions of the people in the first three rows, whom Oceana obviously had done a lot of deep healing work for. Oceana suddenly walked down our row as they spoke to the crowd, and they stopped right in front of me. I looked up at them, and they looked down at me, and they said, 'Hi, Al.' And my heart and chest area exploded into what seemed like a million pieces! At the time, I had no idea what had just happened. Oceana asked me if I wanted to say anything as I sat there in shock. I said no, but then decided to not be such a coward and asked them, 'How do you remember me?' I didn't know how they could pick me out of a big crowd like that after only a thirty-minute session with me a year and a half before that. Oceana said, 'How do we remember you? We could tell you everything about your last twenty lives.' I had never really heard about past lives, and that really got my attention. I began to go to their classes, and soon I was taking their one-year course. During the course, my heart opened, and I had grown so much that I wanted to naturally give back and offered to help set up the nonprofit school they were planning—the Oceanic Institute—in 1991, which is now called the Oceana Light Foundation. I fully enjoyed every minute of helping run the school. At an Oceana meditation retreat in Estes Park, Colorado, in 1993, while Amritam was leading a breath session for all the participants, I had an experience of what seemed like Divine forgiveness of the ego and all of my actions throughout my lifetimes. Divine light melted my ego away like a snowflake on a warm windshield ... poof! Simultaneously, the realization that nothing had ever really happened to me or anyone else, as we were all in a dream, dawned on my consciousness, and that we are all in the same boat, thinking that everything was real, and we had done something wrong in the past that we were trying to make up for. I felt totally forgiven and redeemed, once and for all, which brought about tremendous healing and compassion for myself and all people. At an Oceana meditation retreat in Hawaii in 1992, Oceana was leading another one of their amazing meditations/visualizations, and suddenly, my crown chakra opened and white light poured through my body, seemingly burning all of my cells and triggering the ancient memory of Divine light as who I really am. As the Divine white light of existence filled my vision, the material world fell away completely. No words can truly describe it. It is an unforgettable experience. In 1998, at Amritam's house in Boulder, Colorado, a group of her students and I were in the kitchen, just cleaning the house, and suddenly, all the content in my consciousness rose out in front of me and I saw it as unreal. It was as if everything in my mind and in the material world had suddenly disappeared ... forgiven once and for all and gone forever (like objects falling off the back of a boat and disappearing into the Ocean)! In its place was the peace and purity of the potential of the universe, or all there is, and the knowing that this peace and purity of the universe is the only thing that is really real. I was stunned. The peaceful aftereffects of this experience are still with me today. In 2013, I mysteriously lost fifty pounds steadily over a fifteen-month period while living in Hawaii. I am five feet ten inches tall and normally weigh 173 pounds, so at 122 pounds, I looked like a skeleton at the time. Quite often, friends would ask me if I was OK, but I never felt physically sick or weak. So I moved back to Boulder, Colorado, to Amritam's Love Peace Harmony Center and met with Oceana regularly. Within eight months, I was back to my normal weight and was helping at her center again. I feel very fortunate and have great gratitude and love for Oceana and Amritam. It is an honor to serve here and give back to humanity. I feel truly blessed to have met Amritam and Oceana and the Twenty-Four, and I can't thank them enough for what they do for me and humanity. I have loved and served Oceana and Amritam for thirty-five years and feel that it has been my calling in life. I can't thank you enough, Amritam and Oceana, for allowing me to serve you, for it has been an honor for me, and I am in deep love and gratitude to you forever!"

Testimonial by Anand Shakti

"I have been studying with Oceana and the Twenty-Four, as well as Amritam, for about twenty-four years. I started meditating at age seventeen, and I am now sixty-eight. I was raised Christian, later lived in a Buddhist monastery, worked with a Gurdjieff group, and did years of therapy. All of that prepared me to come and study with live masters who can interact with me. That is a very different issue than studying the words of a great master. To have enlightened beings present to guide me through every issue that needs unraveling is amazing beyond words. I definitely grew in those earlier times, but these twenty-four years have been an entirely different experience. I came into this life to pretty good parents, but I brought with me a decent amount of emotional and mental clutter that needed resolving. Most of it I had no idea about. With the guidance of Amritam, Oceana, and all the enlightened beings she channels and invites here, every aspect of my life changed. I am way happier, healthier, wealthier, caring, loving, and smarter too. Of course, it hasn't always been easy. Change is tough sometimes, but it gets easier the less fear and protection I carry around with me. I've dealt with every powerful emotion possible, so this is not spiritual bypass. This is the real thing, and I love it. I will give you one example of many of the help I have received. I was sitting in class with Oceana about ten years ago. My work life had improved, but not to anything I really loved yet. They looked at me and said very directly, 'Please, please, please get certified in massage.' I don't know that Oceana generally does that kind of thing. I haven't bumped into it since, but I had tears running down my face. I didn't know why. I had just had a bout of double pneumonia and had borrowed money from my family and friends to keep me afloat until I could work again. I was self-employed. I can say that I was terrified. Financially, it was a huge leap, and I had been doing my own little thing, being the good spiritual student and staying low, so doing this at age fifty-eight was seriously scary for me. The truth is, after so many years of listening to their help and guidance, I did it. They'd only helped me in all those years, and I trusted them. I felt like I was flying through the air, and I was not comfortable. Petrified is more like it. I started having the best years of my life. I loved the massage school (Healing

Spirits), loved massage, and loved having new friends. Now, nine years later, I am loving what I do and I have wonderful clients. I am always learning more about how to open myself to be guided to truly helping them. My life is more rounded in every way, and I can once again bring more of my focus back to the Divine. This is the life ... as they say!"

Testimonial by Satya Mary, "Thoughts on Having a Spiritual Teacher (or Two or Three)"

"I am glad I have a spiritual teacher. Actually, I have more than one. I read a book that said when the student is ready the teacher will appear. It was a book about meditation. And, sure enough, that's what happened. First it was Sun Bear. I learned through him and many other spiritual Native American teachers how to honor and receive messages from 'all my relations' in the other kingdoms. These teachers, in turn, led me to Oceana and the Twenty-Four when I was ready for the next step. Amritam was the person who channeled Oceana. When I first sat on the floor on a *zafu* to listen to Oceana, the hairs on the back of my neck and on my arms stood up. I knew I was hearing the absolute truth. There were no ifs, ands, buts, maybes, or doubts about it. Their message was about responsibility: 'Responding in the here and now, with love for yourself first and then anyone else in any given situation.' It was about forgiveness: 'One has to forgive their parents, God, anyone else who has ever hurt them, and themselves.' It was about anger: 'We all carry a certain amount of rage, because deep down, we all know there is more to life than what we were taught, and nobody is telling us what that is.' 'There is no real time but now. The past is memories; the future is imagination. You can only respond in the now.' (When the future arrives, it will be the now). 'Your mind/ego's job is to protect your life. To get you to get out of the way if a truck is coming. It is not concerned with your soul's enlightenment. It isn't meant to guide you through life.' It turns out that who I am—my true self, deep down inside—is not my mind nor my body nor my personal identity principles and deeds. It's much bigger than that. In meditation, sometimes all of that dissolves, and yet I am blissfully conscious of being aware and an intrinsic part of the lack of all that. Nothing much happens overnight most of the time. With consistent meditation, chanting, mystic dance, Divine energy transmissions, spiritual dialogue, breath work, and living in community with like-minded souls, etc., life took on new meaning, and I experienced life in a different light, literally and figuratively. My soul journey involves removing gunk from the facet of the diamond that represents me. The diamond being the one consciousness that alone is and includes all of us. As I worked on removing the gunk that diminishes the light wanting to shine through my facet, I become more of a vehicle of light of the vast consciousness, not of my head. Amritam as a spiritual teacher has the job of facilitating this purification for her students. It's not an easy job. One's ego mind and their soul are often in different boats and end up going to battle with each other like pirate ships versus the ships bearing gold, over and over again, believe me. And one's spiritual teacher can see what's happening for you but often can only hold you in a space of encouragement and light. If they say what they see before you get it yourself, they can incur the student's wrath, and then the battle suddenly externalizes against the teacher. It is a job that requires vast reserves of love, patience, perseverance, dedication, and discernment. Smattered with plenty of trust and a sense of humor, I think. Amritam has been truly amazing at fulfilling this role in my life and the lives of others. And it's amazing, too, to discover the layers and layers one's facet's gunk can actually have. Amritam has been a channel for Oceana, and since 2006, if I remember correctly, of other high spiritual masters and divine saints of several traditions as well. Having had an experience of 'oneness with all' back in the '70s (that no one was able to answer her questions about at the time), she carries within the desire to have a center someday for teachers and masters to come and to share the truth of oneness with people like you and me. The world needs it. People are yearning for it and often run around the supposed 'real' world wondering, 'What the hell?' and, 'Where do I fit in?' or, 'Do I really want to fit in, in all of this?' In 2001, Amritam's dream came to fruition and she acquired land with a red barn that soon became Baba's barn and later was dedicated as Master Sha's first Love, Peace, Harmony Center. A place of healing, a place of learning, a refuge for the soul, a place where many spiritual teachers have come, a place dedicated to oneness. I have traveled to India with Amritam and her other students where, true to her belief in oneness and her soul purity, we were able to visit three ashrams and meet other spiritual teachers. More recently, we have been blessed to have met Master Sha through Amritam's continued soul journey and her desire to help others on their soul journeys. She is a very humble person and does not believe in hoarding her students all to herself. I have studied with and been bestowed with soul healing treasures by Master Sha, and I consider my life to be extraordinary as a result. I have learned to sing my soul song, communicate with other souls, heal through divine intervention and love, and honor and have compassion for others and myself. The last one is the hardest for me, but as I said, I am a work in progress. That's why I have a spiritual teacher, or more than one. I still have bouts of wanting to run away and 'do my thing' as a rugged individualist at times, but I also know that would be a case of the blind leading the blind, however smart I might think I am. After all, I am one of those who originally resonated with Oceana's statement back in 1993 that we recognize there is a much bigger picture happening for all of us than you hear about in everyday life. And I choose to live in the light, not the darkness. Ignorance, in my case, was not bliss. Meditation for me was/is (sometimes). So I choose that, and to live in love, peace, and harmony with everyone else in the vastness of the oneness that we all are. I choose to heal myself and others. It's my newest way toward changing the world for the better. It's an ongoing process, and I love it."

Testimonial by Dyvin Heart

"For nearly three decades I have been a student of Amritam and Oceana; and during this time, my view and understanding of existence (or life) and myself has changed so much. I thought my body, thoughts, and feelings were the only things that really existed. I did not know about my soul or about spirituality. Every time I would see Amritam and Oceana, I would experience a new understanding of life, about me, and how we are all connected. How I think, what I do, what I say affects all of existence. I also realize that how I see and think about myself affects what kind of life I will have. I have become aware that I had put myself in a cage by my limited thinking, and that cage was not created by others but by me. And, because I was the creator of that cage, I am the one who can open that cage and my limited thinking and be free to explore the world in a new way. I am not bound by my past, nor do I fear the future. I am just in this moment seeing what is truly before me. Knowing that I created this moment for a learning and a new experience. Why have I stayed as a student with Amritam and Oceana for so long? It is because I continue to see life and myself in new and expanded ways. I am not bound by the experiences of the past. I just see them as learning tools for learning and to have prepared me for this precious moment."

Testimonial by Barbara Wunsch

"Approximately eighteen years ago I was blessed and fortunate to meet Amritam and Oceana. During this time of personal growth I have been supported with love, intelligence, and integrity. When it came time to make a wise decision, they would bring me to the wisest path, uplifting me to a higher awakening. I was taught many forms of meditation that brought me to a deeper awareness and understanding through movement, chanting, and being of service. They encouraged and supported me to become a better person for myself and others. It has been a life of inspiration, love, and joy that has continued to deepen my understanding. Through Oceana and Amritam's teachings of oneness this has made my travels at home and abroad a closeness to all that is and filled my heart with a deeper love for humanity and this beautiful planet we live on. In bringing many teachers and types of education, I had the foundation to grow in love, forgiveness, compassion, and wisdom. Oceana and Amritam have been there to bring clarity and love to any situation offering healing and many blessings. As I traveled, their wisdom, love, and beauty have always been with me. I am so grateful for these tremendous and wondrous blessings in my life. Thank you, thank you, thank you."

Testimonial by Kip Golden

"I met Amritam and Oceana when I was eighteen or nineteen. I was a fragile, insecure, and shut-down young man. This was the simple truth of how I came to her. I seemed normal on the surface, but underneath was the me who knew I had come into this world quite confident and full of zest for life and had since shut down. I yearned deeply to fly again, like a lost child wants to go home. I had no idea how to get there. Although my family meant well, they had no idea how to help me. Amritam and Oceana were my saving grace as I did everything they offered (classes). I gained the knowledge that we are all of divinity, and that all and everything is from the same infinite consciousness. I felt the dignity that gave me and all things, whether small and seemingly unimportant or big and important. I had several profound experiences. Amritam rebirthed me on a retreat in Italy in a way which resulted in me laying on the floor in the greatest warm bliss I had ever felt, incomparable to anything I knew to be possible. Another time, I meditated half the night until I was in such a space that, even when I tried, I couldn't possibly remember what I could ever be afraid of. I knew beyond doubt that the true me, my spirit, was immortal and happy. I met many masters whose teachings she included into her trainings, all of whom blessed me. She married my wife, Kim, and I; and then later, my two beautiful boys were incredibly blessed by Master Sha, a master she brought us to and the most powerful healer I had ever met. At one point, I lived in San Francisco where every day at 6:00 a.m. on my train ride to work for at least six months straight, I did an exquisite visualization that Oceana had done for me to reprogram my subconscious mind. I can't explain it, but I could feel my cells changing with that infusion of light and love every single day that I did that. All of this helped me to peel away the layers of insecurity and confusion that had prevented me from experiencing the brave, shiny me. My spiritual mother Amritam (and Oceana) was/is the best long-term guide on the spiritual path I could ever ask for! At one point, after so much inner transformation, she could see I was still hesitating in fear. She looked at me and said, 'What are you waiting for? You're capable, handsome, and intelligent. Only you are stopping you from living an incredible life.' She had a way of being grounded, real, human, and compassionate in the moment I needed to hear her truthful statements the most. That particular one changed my life. Today, although my journey of discovery continues, I am at last empowered with confidence and the passion for life that I lacked since my childhood. In addition, I have a deep love of the Divine (and my teachers) that continually blesses my life. Now the possibilities are endless!"

Testimonial by Ginette Morin

"The wisdom imbued with love and light touches my heart and enlightens my mind. Thank you, Oceana and Amritam, for the upliftment, happiness, and magic that you bring. With love, Ginette."

— CHAPTER 13 —

Oceana Divine Meditations

Oceana's Meditation for the New Year (12/28/2018)

Dear beloved ones, this is Oceana. The new year has come to you. This is wonderful because now, in the new year, you have all learned new things from the last year and just know you can create whatever you would like. You can create new jobs and new relationships, and this is very wonderful to start brand-new. All of you who want to create new things and ways to bring new people to you and abundance to your work and things you love to do, it's so wonderful to start new. You have learned all kinds of new things last year. So go forward and create your new dreams, new relationships, and new friends. Don't forget to start your meditations every day now, brand-new. This will bring great new ideas, and it will allow you to be more creative. So go for it, everybody! It's a good year. We send lots of love and light to all of you. So go for it. Do all your dreams; it will be wonderful! We are sending love to all of you. Remember, you can create whatever you love and want. You have all been meditating, so continue to meditate and to create your dreams. This year is going to bring abundance to everyone, so just keep doing what you love, and you will have a great new year. This is Oceana and the Twenty-Four sending blessings, love, abundance, and new ideas for all of you. Just remember to meditate, and you will get all the answers you need. We will send messages once in a while to help you create joy and happiness in your life. With love, Oceana and the Twenty-Four, trance-channeled by Amritam.

Oceana's Special Holiday Meditation (11/29/2018)

Dear beloved ones, this is the special holiday season for all of you. It is such a beautiful time on your Earth. Make sure you open your heart with love and light, and meditate every day, and just celebrate the Divine! Every day, you can do a small meditation. This is how you do it: When you wake in the morning, you just thank the Divine for your beautiful morning, and have a beautiful day with your family and friends. And every night, you can thank the Divine for your beautiful day. We love you, and we celebrate you. Have a great time during your holidays! With love, Oceana and the Twenty-Four, trance-channeled by Amritam.

Oceana's "You Are a Light Being" Meditation (10/25/2018)

Dear everyone, you are all beautiful light beings. You were all born here on this Earth and came here to learn and grow and understand the people on the Earth. This was also for all of you to go in and meditate and learn how the human beings are beautiful and have come to realize the Divine is always with them! We send love and light to everyone! With love, Oceana and the Twenty-Four, trance-channeled by Amritam.

Oceana's Fall Season Meditation (9/28/2018)

Dearest ones, it is the fall season. In the fall season, it is time to go in and meditate. When you meditate, you feel the love of the Divine. As the new season comes, everyone will see the beautiful colors as the plants change to orange, red, and yellow; and it brings happiness, peace, and beauty to the people. So, everyone, just remember to meditate and open your heart as you watch the season and colors change. Everything will be so beautiful. We send love, joy, and happiness to all of you from Oceana and the Twenty-Four. With love, Oceana and the Twenty-Four, trance-channeled by Amritam.

Oceana's Rainbow Light of Love Meditation (8/27/2018)

Dearest ones, it is very beautiful that you are all beginning to meditate, and you are doing your meditations in the morning and evening. We are so happy that you have started to meditate. Know that we are always with you, and the Divine is always with you. As you read this message, just imagine that the Divine is surrounding you with golden light. As you sit there, you say, "Dear Divine, thank you for all your love. We are so happy to sit in meditation." Dear ones, we are glad you are meditating.

Oceana is sending beautiful golden light to all of you. Just close your eyes, and you will feel a beautiful rainbow come around. Just call my name, "Oceana, Oceana, Oceana," and I will come with beautiful rainbow light to surround you with peace, love, and happiness. Just remember to close your eyes at night, and thank the rainbow light of love to continue to surround you all through the night. You are all loved by all the ancient beings of peace and joy. They will surround you with peace, joy, and love through the night as you sleep. Have a beautiful meditation when you read this message! With love, Oceana and the Twenty-Four, trance-channeled by Amritam.

Oceana's "The Divine Is Always with You" Meditation (7/31/2018)

My dearest ones, this is Oceana. We send love to all. Just know that you are all loved; and if you listen to this message, just close your eyes. We are the ones that send love, peace, and harmony to all of you. So, every morning, just know when you wake up that we are there, and just say, "Dear Divine, send me love, joy, happiness, peace, and abundance." And we will send you love, joy, happiness, peace, and abundance. We are always with you ... Love, love, love, love. Have a beautiful day! And just know that we are always near you. Just call our name three times ..., "Divine, Divine, Divine, please come"! With love, Oceana and the Twenty-Four, trance-channeled by Amritam.

Oceana's "Love to the Divine" Meditation (6/26/2018)

Dear ones, this is Oceana and the Twenty-Four. We are sending joy, love, and peace to each of you. Just close your eyes every morning and tell the Divine you love them, and feel the golden light surround you with peace, love, and harmony. Just ask the Divine to continue to send love and light, and thank them for their love and joy. They are always with you. With love, Oceana and the Twenty-Four, trance-channeled by Amritam.

Oceana's "Love from the Absolute" Divine Meditation (5/30/2018)

I am the one who brings peace, joy, and harmony. It is time for the people on the Earth to go in and open the hearts of all people. This will be a very big job, but the ancient ones have all come together to give each of you joy, love, peace, and abundance. When you all are in that space, your world and all of you will open your hearts to all of you. So, everyone, go inside and feel the love coming to the Earth from the great ones who are sending love, peace, harmony, and joy. Your Earth is going to celebrate again. We love you, and we will give you more information so that all the people on your Earth will remember. The ancient ones will come through dreams and give joy and abundance to all those on the Earth who will start to remember that everyone on the Earth is one. Beautiful, joyous peace will come to all of you. It will take a little time, but all the old ancient ones are sending peace to all of you, all countries, all people; and slowly, the Earth will become one beautiful, golden light of love for all people.

So, those of you who are reading this, just close your eyes and say, "Golden light, please come heal me, heal my family, heal the Earth, and heal all countries."

And all people, remember, you are all one beautiful presence of the Absolute. You are all loved. We have not forgotten you. All of you, dear ones, forgive all of your friends and people, and then you will remember you are one with the Absolute. We send peace, joy, and love to all of you. Just know that the ancient ones are coming with love, joy, peace, and harmony. In time, in the next few years, your Earth will be given high consciousness to all of you. Then the Earth will bring abundance, healing, peace, and gifts from the Absolute to all people, for you are all loved. With that, we send love, peace, harmony, abundance, health, healing, and joy that will come to all of you. Right now, you can even feel the celebration in your heart. Love to all of you from the Absolute. With love from the Absolute, and Oceana and the Twenty-Four, trance-channeled by Amritam.

Oceana's "Spring Is Here" Divine Meditation (4/23/2018)

Dearest ones, this is Oceana and the Twenty-Four. The beautiful spring has come. This is a new beginning for all of you. So the Divine is going to ask all of you to meditate in the morning and the evening. So just close your eyes. And ask the Divine to surround you with beauty, love, and abundance. As you sit there, you will feel the beauty of yourself and your world. When you meditate, you feel happy and joyous for your beautiful life. If you have any problems, just ask the Divine to bless you with peace, joy, and love. So, every day, when you close your eyes, just ask the Divine to surround you with love, joy, peace, and harmony for your life. And the Divine may give you a message. So just keep a sheet of paper by you so you can get your message from the Divine. We love you. Enjoy your life. Be kind to others. And meditate so the Divine can give you new beginnings. You are all loved.

Spring is here. You can create new and wonderful ideas and friends, and new things to come to you in your new beginning of spring. You are all loved. Don't forget to love yourself and others. This is the time to plant new ideas and new beginnings; just like when you plant a beautiful flower, you take care of it and feed it, so create joy and happiness. Now do that for yourself, for you are loved by all there is. The Divine is always with you. We send you love, peace, harmony, joy, and wonderment. Keep creating new and wonderful things for yourself and others. This is from Oceana and the Twenty-Four, sending you blessings, joy, abundance, and happiness for the new spring. Have a wonderful day! With love, Oceana and the Twenty-Four, trance-channeled by Amritam.

Oceana's "Calling the Divine to You" Meditation (3/20/2018)

Dearest ones, this is Oceana. We are sending you a meditation. We are so happy to send this message to you. Just know that the Divine and all the saints are sending all of you love, healing, and peace. We are so happy that you are all starting to meditate again. When you meditate, just say, "Dear Divine, thank you for sending love, peace, harmony, and joy." Just remember that the Divine is always with you. Just thank the Divine from your heart, and you will feel a beautiful, soft, healing light all around you. We love you, dear ones. Just keep meditating, and keep calling the Divine to you. Then close your eyes, and you will feel beautiful love coming to you. With love from Oceana and the Twenty-Four, trance-channeled by Amritam.

Oceana's "Thank the Divine" Meditation (2/26/2018)

Dearest ones, this is Oceana. We are sending you a meditation. When you awake in the morning, just sit and ask the Divine to surround you with golden light. You tell the Divine that you love them and honor them, and that you want to thank them for all their love. As you sit there, you will feel a beautiful light come around you, and you'll just say, "Thank you, Divine, for all your love." Just say, "Thank you for all the gifts you have given me, dear Divine." With love from Oceana and the Twenty-Four, trance-channeled by Amritam.

Oceana's "Open Your Heart to the Divine Sunset" Meditation (1/28/2018)

Dearest ones, this is Oceana and the Twenty-Four. We are looking outside, and as your sun goes down, it is so beautiful. Your world starts with the sun rising, and in the evening your sun goes down. That is a time to allow yourself to do whatever it is you want to do and enjoy the peace of the end of the day. As the sun leaves you, just open your heart and thank the Divine to send you love, peace, harmony, and maybe new ideas; enjoy your life. We love you and know you can create whatever you want in your life. With love from Oceana and the Twenty-Four, trance-channeled by Amritam.

Oceana and the Twenty-Four's "Happy New Year" Divine Meditation (12/30/2017)

Beloved ones, this is Oceana and the Twenty-Four. We are sending a beautiful light of peace, love, and harmony to all of you for your new year. When you get this message, just sit down and say, "Dear Divine, I love you."

This is Oceana, the Twenty-Four, and the Divine Beings of all there is sending joy, happiness, abundance, and peace to all of you. We send a wonderful, joyous year for you for the next year! So, on your New Year's Eve, just say, "Dear Oceana and the Twenty-Four, thank you for everything." We love you, and we care for you, so celebrate the new year, for you will create wonderful magic in your life in the new year. For those of you who have plans and dreams to create wonderful things, this is the year to do it! We send blessings to you. Oceana and the Twenty-Four are always with you,and we are also celebrating your new year. We wish you new beginnings and a new, wonderful year for yourself, your family, and your friends ... celebrate, celebrate, celebrate with love, joy,and happiness.

Just know the Divine is always with all of you. Have a great new year! Just close your eyes, and the Divine will give you love, joy, happiness, and peace in the new year! Love to all from Oceana and the Twenty-Four and the Divine, trance-channeled by Amritam.

Oceana and the Twenty-Four's "Crystal Light" Divine Meditation (11/28/2017)

Beloved ones, this is Oceana. I am giving you a meditation to do in the morning or night, or at any time. This is called the "Crystal Light" meditation. You can do it in the morning and night, or whenever it is needed.

So just sit down close your eyes, and ask the Divine to send crystal light all around you. So you just sit and close your eyes and say, "Please, crystal light, come and surround me with your light." The crystal light will surround you and send waves of love, peace, and harmony. Then you say, "Crystal light, I love you. Please send love and light to my soul with joy, abundance, and happiness." Then you just send crystal light and love to your families and friends; and when you do that, they will feel the love coming to them. Also, when you send the love, send the love with abundance and peace.

With love from Oceana and the Twenty-Four, trance-channeled by Amritam.

Oceana and the Twenty-Four's "Golden and Purple Light" Divine Meditation (10/25/2017)

Dear beloveds, this is Oceana and the Twenty-Four. We are sending our love to you. There are twenty-four beings in our group that carry beautiful light, caring, and joy. We are sending beautiful love and light from the Twenty-Four to all of you who are reading this.

Just close your eyes and ask the Divine to surround you in beautiful golden and purple light. Just sit down and feel the love of the golden and purple light surrounding you with peace, love, harmony, and joy in your heart. They love you so much, and they are surrounding you with this beautiful light. So, when you sit down, just call the light and say, "Please come and bless me and my family and friends." We love you. Have a beautiful day! With love from Oceana and the Twenty-Four, trance-channeled by Amritam.

Oceana's "Loving the Earth" Divine Meditation (9/30/2017)

Dear ones, this is Oceana. I will give you a beautiful meditation that you can do every morning or night. This meditation is a meditation of love, peace, and harmony for your Earth. Whenever you do this meditation, just find a quiet space outside to see the beauty of your Earth.

Now, dear ones, just close your eyes. This is a meditation for you to sit and give your love and caring and to share how much you are grateful for your Earth and where you live and the beauty of the mountains, deserts, oceans, forests, rivers, animals, trees, and flowers and the beauty of your land. So, every morning, just awaken, and thank your Earth for its love and beauty and that it feeds you, blesses you, and creates beautiful places to live.

So many of you are awakening in consciousness and you are connecting with the Divine, connecting with love of all there is. Just know that the Divine is always with you; every time you do your prayer, they are in great gratitude for your love ... love of the land, the people, and the joy and happiness where you are, where there are no wars and no worries. Open your heart and ask the Divine to balance you mentally, physically, and emotionally. Thank the Divine for all the gifts you have received. This way, you become one with the Divine, and your world becomes balanced. As you open your heart, love the land, the mountains, the rivers, the trees, and the oceans, for your Earth is beautiful. Just keep raising your consciousness and loving the people, for your Earth is amazing! Thank the Divine for this amazing place you have to live in. Just keep loving each other, learning from each other, and creating a beautiful world of love, peace, and harmony. Every day, just send your love to the land, oceans, atmosphere, people, and children and ask that everything stay balanced mentally, physically, and emotionally with God's love.

Your Earth is rising in beautiful consciousness, so keep moving forward, keep coming together, keep celebrating, and keep balancing those who need to learn to love again. Oceana is sending golden love and light to your Earth. Just call the golden light, and ask them to send the golden light to your family, friends, and governments. Just keep sending joy, love, and light to everyone to keep you all balanced.

This is from Oceana and the Twenty-Four and all the different ancient ones sending love to your Earth. Have a beautiful day! With love from Oceana and the Twenty-Four, trance-channeled by Amritam.

Oceana's "Divine Love" Meditation (8/30/2017)

Dear ones, this is Oceana. We are sending you love and peace and are opening your heart. Just close your eyes. Call the Divine three times: "Divine, Divine, Divine." Then thank the Divine for all their gifts and all their love, and thank them for helping you raise your consciousness. When you sit down to meditate, close your eyes and ask the angels to surround you with love, peace, and harmony. Then thank them, and you will know you are loved, and the beautiful Divine Beings will send you golden light and peace. With love from Oceana and the Twenty-Four, trance-channeled by Amritam.

Oceana's "Divine Purple Light" Evening Meditation (7/31/2017)

Dear ones, this is Oceana and the Twenty-Four. I am giving you an evening meditation. It will help you relax and let go of your day so you can rest beautifully when you sleep.

Dear ones, this is a meditation for you to go into your heart and relax and feel the love of all there is. When you get ready to do your meditation in the evening, just relax in a beautiful place, close your eyes, and ask the purple light of love to surround you in peace, love, and harmony for your body, heart, and soul. Just relax, close your eyes, and feel the purple light of the Divine surround you. When you call them to surround you in purple light, you will relax and you will feel the love of all there is. Then you will know that the Divine is always with you. Just say, "Divine, Divine, Divine, please come to me and surround me in beautiful purple light." When you feel the purple light, take three deep breaths, relax, and feel the love of the purple light relaxing you, and know that it will surround you through the night. Just say, "Dear purple light, surround me through the night so that I can rest in the arms of God's purple light." Just close your eyes, and know that the Divine is always with you and the purple light holds you in love while you sleep. Just say, "Purple light, purple light, purple light, surround me through the night with love and peace," and then you will rest. With love to you all from Oceana and the Twenty-Four, trance-channeled by Amritam.

Oceana's "Open Your Heart" Divine Morning Meditation (6/21/2017)

Dear ones, this is Oceana and the Twenty-Four. It's time to go inside to your heart and the Divine. Every morning before you get up, just sit and close your eyes. Just call the Divine to come sit with you; open your heart, relax, and visualize your day with joy, love, and happiness.

With love from Oceana and the Twenty-Four, trance-channeled by Amritam.

Oceana's "Love and Light and Balance" Divine Meditation (4/30/2017)

Dearest ones, this is Oceana and the Twenty-Four. It is a very important time. We are calling you, and I have special meditations that I am going to do for you all, and they will be on CDs for you to listen to.

This is a beautiful time because you can go into the world and meditate deeply now. When you meditate deeply, your whole soul glows with love and light. Every time you meditate, the Divine is with you. You are never alone. So, for those of you who are meditators and love to sit with the Divine, this is a very special time.

All kinds of changes are happening in your Earth. But it is a celebration of your Earth, for your Earth is rising in consciousness, love, and caring. Remember that the Divine is always with you. Oceana and the Twenty-Four are always with you. Just call the Divine's name and they will answer your questions and send blessings. The Twenty-Four have come to the Earth to balance the energies of love, light, and healing. Every day, we send love and light and balance to your Earth.

So know that we are always with you and we love you. Call our name three times: "Oceana, Oceana, Oceana" … and we will always send love and light to you.

Have a beautiful meditation tonight. Call my name—Oceana—and I will send beautiful love to you. Then just close your eyes and be in the arms of the Divine as you sleep. We love you. Have a beautiful evening! With love from Oceana and the Twenty-Four, trance-channeled by Amritam.

Oceana's "Spring Has Sprung" Divine Meditation (3/31/2017)

Dear ones, you know it is spring, and it is a birth of new beginnings! It really is true; when you think about spring, the beautiful plants are coming up from the ground and the seeds that were planted from the past are opening. It's such a beautiful time. You can create so many new things in your life.

Every morning, just relax. Close your eyes. Feel spring coming with beautiful new ways to create new things to plant. It's like you get to start over again, and you have learned from the past. Now you are creating new ideas for your life. You can bloom again with new ideas. Gather friends to come to a party or meditation to start brand-new. This is what is so beautiful about spring. You have new beginnings. You can feel the love all around the plants and the trees. Everything has been asleep, and now you are waking up. With new ideas you can meet new friends and you can create wonderful things for your life.

So enjoy the spring, the beauty, and the feeling of love as everything is being born again. Don't forget to dance, because spring has sprung! You can create whatever you like. This is beautiful. You get to start over again. Just send your love to your friends and your family, and begin brand-new. This is great! Spring has sprung ... Yay! Have a good time! With love from Oceana and the Twenty-Four, trance-channeled by Amritam.

Oceana's "Dance with the Divine" Meditation (2/23/2017)

Dearest ones, this is Oceana and the Twenty-Four. I will give a meditation. Just close your eyes, relax your body, and put on beautiful music that you can dance to and move your body to. Just let go in the dance and open your heart to the Divine. Then ask the Divine to sit with you. For when you dance you relax. So remember to dance with the Divine, and then sit in meditation.

Just relax. Call the Divine to come three times. Say, "Please, Divine, come sit with me and meditate with me. I love you." Just meditate in the morning and the evening. Just sit with the Divine and feel the golden light around you. Ask the golden light of the Divine to balance you, to love you, to allow you to receive abundance, to receive love, and to enjoy your life in celebration. At the end of the meditation, just put on beautiful music and dance. Then thank the Divine for their love and sit quietly for five minutes. With love from Oceana and the Twenty-Four, trance-channeled by Amritam.

Oceana's "Love, Light, and Protection" Blessing and Divine Meditation (1/27/2017)

Dear beloveds, this is Oceana and the Twenty-Four. We are sending you beautiful light. Each of you who read this message, just say, "Dear Oceana and the Twenty-Four, please come and give me blessings and protection." Know that we love you and honor you and are always sending love and light to each of you.

Just call our name three times: "Oceana, Oceana, Oceana," and we will send you love and light. Have a beautiful week. We love you and honor you. Remember to call our name three times, and we will send you love and protection. With love from Oceana and the Twenty-Four, trance-channeled by Amritam.

Oceana's "New Year, Golden Light" Divine Meditation (12/29/2016)

Dear beloved ones, this is Oceana. I would love to give you a meditation for your new year. Just go into meditation, beloved ones. Close your eyes. Call the Divine three times. Say, "Dear beloved Divine, dear beloved Divine, dear beloved Divine, please come. I love you."

I've come because you called me, dear ones. Close your eyes. Relax. I will send a golden light around you. You will feel the love. You will feel the love and joy of your new beginnings. We are all sending you love from the soul world. Just keep meditating. Ask the Divine to come. Feel the golden light around you. The Divine loves all of you. This golden light will balance you mentally, physically, and emotionally. The golden light moves into your body, and you feel tremendous love. We are with you. We are celebrating your new year. Allow your dreams and hopes to be created this year, for this is a magical time. You all have beautiful hearts. You love humanity.

Sit in meditation, and the Divine will come and help you create this new year. You are loved beyond words. Just keep your heart open, and you will be given beautiful messages for your new beginnings. It will be a very good year. We love you all. All the saints and all the beings of light send all their love to each of you. We love you dearly. Have a beautiful new year! This is the Divine. Love you, love you, love you. With love from Oceana and the Twenty-Four, trance-channeled by Amritam.

Oceana's "Celebrate Your Life" Divine Meditation (12/6/2016)

Dear beloveds, this is Oceana and the Twenty-Four. Dear ones, know that you are loved and that we will ask you to call in an angel named Sue-La and another angel called Light.

Just sit down, close your eyes, and call Sue-La's name three times, and then call Light's name three times. Then close your eyes, and ask for their blessings, and feel the love around you. You will feel a golden ball of light surrounding you, healing you, and balancing you mentally, physically, and emotionally. As you feel the golden light around you, know that the Divine is hugging you, balancing you, and caring for you. Then just meditate, and if you feel you want to, get up and just dance.

Celebrate your life, and celebrate love of yourself and others. Then thank the Divine and God and ask for blessings. With love from Oceana and the Twenty-Four, trance-channeled by Amritam.

Oceana's "Crystalline Light: Mental, Physical, and Emotional Balance" Divine Meditation (11/11/2016)

Beloved ones, this is Oceana and the Twenty-Four. We come from the land of pure love, light, abundance, and joy.

We are sending the most beautiful crystalline light to each person. This crystalline light will go to your heart. You just touch your chest three times and you will feel a burst of love come through your body. This will balance you mentally, physically, and emotionally. Call our name—Oceana—three times, and we will send you pure love, and you will relax in your life. Thank the Divine and all there is from your heart, and your life will carry joy, abundance, love, and happiness within your soul. Also, you will be able to support and help others.

We love you. We honor you. And we will always send love to you. Have a beautiful, beautiful life. You are blessed! With love from Oceana and the Twenty-Four, trance-channeled by Amritam.

Oceana's "Awaken to Your Inner Consciousness and Light" Divine Meditation (10/24/2016)

Dear ones, this is a message from the spiritual light force of love. We (Oceana and the Twenty-Four) have been raised to this higher vibration of light in the soul world, and we are now in charge of this group that is here to help humanity. We have already told you that love is the answer. You are all carrying God's love in your heart. Just remember to tap three times on your heart. Just call God's name three times, and ask the Divine to remove blockages that are in the way of your heart opening. Remember, it is a great honor to open your heart and love to the Absolute. Take advantage of this time to awaken. The doorways are opening on your Earth now.

Dear ones, this is your time to wake up and get enlightened! We want you to go into your being and your soul and your inner love and light. That's where your inner power and magic are! It's time now to leave the past behind, and forgive those who've hurt you and forgive yourself for those whom you have hurt.

The Divine is close now, and you can awaken. Make sure you meditate every day. There will be gifts given to you. We will help you. It's very important to make time for meditation and inner classes with Oceana. This will help all of you to experience the Divine within you and outside of you. We have never been able to offer upliftments that help you raise your vibration like this ever before. It's now time. Don't waste your time. Please come spend time with us! It's time to awaken to your inner soul and beauty and allow the Divine to erupt the love and light within you. So don't delay. It's really important, dear ones. There are energy fields on your Earth right now that can help you raise your vibration, which will lead you to enlightenment. This only happens every hundred years when the doors open to become enlightened.

Remember, you need to serve humanity, your friends, and your family. With love from Oceana and the Twenty-Four, trance-channeled by Amritam.

Oceana's "Love Is the Answer" Divine Meditation (10/12/2016)

Dear beloveds, this is Oceana. I am here to awaken all of you to open your hearts and send love to yourselves and to all your friends and other people. Love is the answer to all things. We are here to remind all of you that when you love your family, your friends, and your Earth, everything will flower in your life. Just close your eyes every day in the morning and night. Feel the love in your heart. As you open your heart again, dear ones, your lives will flower with love of a beloved, with friends, and with abundance; each day is a new day of love.

Come, all you people, this is Oceana. We have come from another dimension to help you all open your hearts and flower again. It's time now, dear ones; it's time. The Divine is calling you to help yourselves, your families, and your friends with love. Love, love, love, love is the answer.

This is Oceana and the Twenty-Four sending you abundance, love, peace, and Harmony. We love you! Thank you! With love from Oceana and the Twenty-Four, trance-channeled by Amritam.

Oceana's "Raise Your Vibration" Divine Meditation (9/27/2016)

Beloved Ones, I have talked to three people this morning, and they all wanted to meditate and raise their vibrations. I had beautiful sessions with them. So I'm going to give you all a message.

Dear ones, you all carry the seed of love from the Divine. It's time now for you all to go into meditation and call forth your inner souls to speak to the Divine. How you do this is by sitting, closing your eyes, and asking the Divine to surround you in golden light. Then relax and say, "Divine, Divine, Divine, I love you. I feel my heart opening. I feel the light of the Divine within me. I thank you, dear Divine, for helping uplift my consciousness. I have deep gratitude. Thank you, thank you, thank you for the message that I heard today. I am with you. I am grateful, and I am one with God. Thank you, Divine."

The Divine said to close your eyes, open your heart, and be grateful to the light, to the planet, to the children, the stars, the moon, and nature. Also, send love and light to your families and tell them you love them. Just feel the light around you and around your families, and send blessings of joy, abundance, and happiness. Do this meditation every day, and everything will flow better. We love you. With love from Oceana and the Twenty-Four, trance-channeled by Amritam.

Oceana's "Full Moon Lunar Eclipse" Divine Meditation (9/16/2016)

Dear ones, this is Oceana. We love you. Just relax and surround yourself with golden light. Ask the golden light to balance you mentally, physically, and emotionally and to bring peace to your heart. Your planet is having a full moon lunar eclipse. So just meditate, relax, and send love to yourself, your family, and your friends, and ask the Divine to bless you all. We love you. This is Oceana and the Twenty-Four. With love from Oceana and the Twenty-Four, trance-channeled by Amritam.

Oceana's "Fall Season: New Beginnings" Divine Meditation (9/13/2016)

Dear beloved ones, this is Oceana. It is so beautiful on your world when everything changes in what you call the fall. This is the time for everyone to go inside and look deeply into their hearts. It is a very creative time of new beginnings and allowing yourself to go into deep meditation. Just sit outside, look toward the mountain, and allow yourself to feel the peace in your heart. Your world is very busy. Take time every day to sit and meditate. Feel the changes of the weather, and go inside and open your heart. Know that the Divine is always with you. Create new beginnings so that you allow yourself to be connected with the Divine.

Just say, "Divine, Divine, Divine, I love you. Help me to be even closer to all there is." Feel the peace in your heart. Thank the Divine for their love. Remember to call my name ("Oceana, Oceana, Oceana") when you need me or when you are meditating! With love from Oceana and the Twenty-Four, trance-channeled by Amritam.

Oceana's "Love, Peace, and Joy" Divine Meditation (9/5/2016)

Dear ones, this is Oceana. We are sending you love. We are suggesting that, every night when you go to bed, you say my name three times ("Oceana, Oceana, Oceana"), and we will send you love, peace, and joy. We love you all. Keep your hearts open. Know that the Divine is always with you. Know that Oceana is always with you. We are sending you happiness, love, and joy. Enjoy your time, for it is always precious. We love you … from Oceana! With love from Oceana and the Twenty-Four, trance-channeled by Amritam.

Oceana's "You Are All Loved by the Divine" Meditation (8/29/2016)

Dear beloved ones, this is Oceana from the Divine. We are sending beautiful light to each of you. As you read this message, we hope this will open your heart.

Each of you are beloved ones. You are loved by the Divine. We are always there with you. Your world is transforming and changing. Those of you who are meditating and who connect with the Divine every day will be able to create beautiful things and abundance in your life. As you open your heart, call the

Divine. They will give you a message. Today's message is that you are all loved. Know that the love is within your heart, soul, mind, and body. Just sit and meditate. Ask the Divine to come. Know that you are loved, and allow yourself to celebrate your life, your family, and your friends. My suggestion is, when you are in the right mood in the morning or evening, put on some beautiful music and just go inside, close your eyes, and call the Divine to you. You will feel the love. You will remember that you are loved by the Divine and that you are not alone. The Divine is always with you. Just call their name ("Dear Divine") three times, and they will come and help you with whatever is happening for you. You will feel their love and their peace, and you will know you are not alone. We are always with you. So, dear ones, put some music on, and dance and feel the light and feel the love from all there is. We love you. Have a beautiful day, and allow the magic to happen! With love from Oceana and the Twenty-Four, trance-channeled by Amritam.

Oceana's "Crown Chakra, Golden Light" Divine Meditation (8/27/2016)

Dear beloved ones, this is a very special day. We are sending your Earth lots of light and love. We are a committee of twenty-four enlightened ones that help the Earth and keep it balanced. So we are sending you this message and a meditation.

If you have some time, just sit and ask the Divine to send golden light through your crown chakra. Just sit and close your eyes and say, "Dear beloved, dear Divine, please send golden light in through my crown chakra and through my whole body." Ask the Divine to balance you mentally, physically, and emotionally. Close your eyes and feel the love, the peace, and the healing from all there is. We love you. We honor you. And just sit, dear ones, and ask the Divine to heal and balance you so that you can have a beautiful, powerful day. With love from Oceana and the Twenty-Four, trance-channeled by Amritam.

Oceana's "Connecting with Your Higher Self" Divine Meditation (8/16/2016)

Beloved ones, this is Oceana. Many of you do know who I am. I've come from a different dimension to support your world and to support my own world. I speak through Amritam, for she is a pure being. I am so happy to be with you all. I am going to give you a way to call your higher self, the enlightened one within you. For those of you who are ready to receive your higher self, you will get the message immediately. For those of you who are just learning to tune in to your higher self, it may take a week or two. I will help you bring your higher self through, if you need that. Amritam has been channeling for thirty years. She has brought me through her, as well as Buddha, Jesus, Mother Mary, Guan Yin, Osho, and many other enlightened ones.

We are sending this message to all of you, to remind you to meditate and to listen to the sound of the Divine. Many of you are ready to receive the Divine's messages to help humanity. Keep your hearts open. Meditate. When you meditate, just close your eyes. Take three or four deep breaths through your mouth. Find a quiet place to sit, where no one will disturb you. Many of you who receive this message have been with me before.

I am calling you to open your hearts again. Forgive the past. Forgive those who've hurt you, and forgive yourself. I am calling you. I'm sending you love and peace, and I am reminding you that you're here on the Earth with Oceana and the Twenty-Four and other great beings. It's time now to wake up. Open your heart. Just sit now in a beautiful place. Take three or four deep breaths with your mouth open. Ask the Divine to come, and you will be given a message from the Divine. Keep your heart open, love yourself, forgive those who've hurt you, and forgive yourself, for it's time to help yourself and humanity. Just close your eyes. Dear ones, ask the Divine to fill you with golden light through your crown chakra. As you meditate, you will feel the golden light go through your crown chakra and balance you mentally, physically, and emotionally. Forgive those who've hurt you, and forgive yourself. Put your hand on your heart and tap it three times, and you will remember why you are here on this Earth to help humanity, your family, and your friends. You carry a beautiful star in your heart. Just close your eyes, tap three times, and you'll receive a beautiful message from the Divine. Make sure you keep a pen and paper nearby.

We love you. The Divine loves you. Your guides love you. It's now time for some of you to write your books to help humanity in the changing times. I love you. For others of you who are healers, open up your practices again and send your love. That's my message for today. I love you, and I will be speaking to you again. With love from Oceana and the Twenty-Four, trance-channeled by Amritam.

A Special Message from Oceana (8/10/2016)

Beloved ones, this is Oceana and the Twenty-Four with a message from the soul world for all of you. We have come to send waves of pure love to all of those who read this message. Each of you carry a seed of God's light. Just put your hand on your heart every morning. You will feel a warmth and joy from the Divine. Just tap your heart three times. Close your eyes, and tap your heart three times. Close your eyes, and know that the Divine is within you and around you. Every day you do this, you will feel joy in your heart. Just ask the Divine to remove all obstacles in the way of your having a more beautiful life. Thank the Divine. Thank your own self, and remember that the Absolute is always with you. Just tap your heart three times whenever you need help, and the Divine will be there. Just remember to open your heart, and everything will start to work. We love you. The Divine loves you. Just speak to the Divine every day, and stay connected, and everything will flow beautifully in your life.

My name, Oceana, means "ocean," which is vast. "Cean" is the wind. "Ana" is the female aspect of the Divine. We come with a cluster of twenty-four beings. We have come to share love and light to each of you. We love you. Have a beautiful day! With love from Oceana and the Twenty-Four, trance-channeled by Amritam.

A Special Message from Oceana (7/31/2016)

My dearest ones, this is Oceana with a message from the soul world for all of you. Each of you carry a beautiful crystalline star within your heart. You were given this beautiful star to call you home when it is time. The time is now to meditate, to forgive those who've hurt you, to love yourself, and to bring forth the joy of the Divine and the love of the Divine to all people. We are always with you. Just keep loving everyone and forgiving everyone. Forgive yourselves, and go inside, dear ones, and ask the Divine to help you and to stay with you and uplift the consciousness of your world. For it is a very magical and precious time in your world. Just close your eyes and visualize your love for your family and friends. Just know that the Divine is always with you. You are all beautiful. Just keep loving each other and the Earth. This will take some time, but we are here to help you open your heart and love again. Dear ones, it's OK to allow your love and light and knowledge to go into the world. Forgive the past, and open your hearts to the here and now and just dance, celebrate, and love your family and friends. Slowly, slowly, your world will come back into balance. The soul world is helping your planet. Just keep meditating, celebrating, and dancing! We love you and we care for you. Have a beautiful day. Remember, the Divine is always with you! With love from Oceana and the Twenty-Four, trance-channeled by Amritam.

A Special Message from Oceana: "Mother Mary" Meditation (7/26/2016)

Dear beloveds, this is Oceana. We are bringing you another meditation message from the soul world. Before you meditate, make sure you create the space. Sit down comfortably wherever you meditate and where you feel safe and can be free from interruptions. Always try to do your meditation at the same time at night and in the morning. This creates a meditation field with love and energy in it. If you do this every night and every morning, you will find yourself much more centered and will feel your heart and love for friends and family and the Divine. When you sit down to meditate, say, "Beloved ones." And, if you have a certain saint you want to call upon, such as Mary, Jesus, your guru, or your meditation teacher, call their name and ask them to sit with you. Find a place where you want to meditate and where there are no disturbances, if possible. Close your eyes, and feel and ask for the cylinder of golden-purple light to surround you in your meditation. You are in a beautiful cylinder of light. Allow yourself to be comfortable. You may want to have beautiful music playing that you love.

Now I am giving you a meditation: Oceana and the soul world are sending you a Divine blessing to balance you mentally, physically, and emotionally. Every morning or night (whichever is better for you), do this meditation. Close your eyes, dear ones. Relax your body. Take three deep breaths. Then relax your whole body. Call my name: "Mother Mary, Mother Mary, Mother Mary, please send light to me." Say this three times. Then you will feel a beautiful golden light around you. Just relax, let go of your day, and ask the Divine to bless you with love, joy, and happiness. This is a message from the Divine. Know that we are always with you. If you do this every day for ten to fifteen minutes (or before bed), you will find that your days will be easier and you will feel much more balanced in your body, heart, and soul. We love you, dear ones. Please do these meditations; they will help you in your life. Also, let us know how your meditations are helping you. If you have an experience, please send it to us and we will share it with people. We love you. Have a beautiful day. With love and light from Oceana and the Twenty-Four, trance-channeled by Amritam.

A Special Divine Meditation from Oceana (7/21/2016)

Beloved ones, this is Oceana. I am giving a meditation. Just close your eyes. Go inside and say, "Dear soul of mine, I love you." Relax your body. Let go of all tension. Imagine that you see a blue light, and you feel it surround you, and you feel deep love. Just relax. You begin to relax your entire being. As you sit there, you feel this beautiful peace in your body. You just let go and breathe. Take three or four deep breaths. Then you feel a deep relaxation. You let go of your worldly life. You ask the Divine to come. You feel a deep peace surrounding you. Everything relaxes. Your whole body relaxes and feels deep peace. You feel as if the most beautiful warm light is surrounding you. You take three more deep breaths, breathing in the light. Then you ask the Divine to heal you or remove any blockages in your life. You feel your whole body fill with light, and you say, "I love you, Divine. I love my friends and family, and I ask the Divine to continue to send love, light, and abundance to my family and friends." And you sit in the space and feel the love that's being given to you by all there is. And you relax … just feel the peace, and you may be given some information or just silence. Just sit in the bliss. You'll know when to come back; and when you do, take deep breaths. Enjoy, dear ones. We love you! With love from Oceana and the Twenty-Four, trance-channeled by Amritam.

Oceana's "Golden Light Forgiveness" Divine Meditation (7/15/16)

A beautiful golden light, a ball of golden light, surrounds your body. This golden light is just around you, and you say, "I love you, golden light. I love my soul, I love my body, I love my heart, I love my masters and my teachers, I love myself, and I am slowly, slowly, slowly awakening to the love of the Absolute. Thank you, God. Thank you, Absolute. Thank you, Divine. Thank you, thank you, thank you. I love you. I love myself, and I love others. I forgive those who have hurt me, and I forgive myself if I have hurt anyone else." Once you do that forgiveness practice, everything opens up. Every time you forgive yourself or people who have hurt you, you are set free ready to walk to the light, to walk into the love, and to walk into the joy of peace, love, and harmony. This is Oceana. I love you all. Thank you for being here. Thank you for listening, and thank you for your beautiful gifts that each of you have given to others and to each other. We are in deep gratitude. You are in deep gratitude for the masters you've met, for the teachers you've met, for the people who've helped you, and for the people you have helped. And you just sit and meditate, and you say, "I love my soul. I love my soul. I am slowly, slowly awakening to pure enlightenment. Thank you, Divine. Thank you, thank you, thank you." Everybody, take a deep breath. (Oceana rings the bell.) All right! With love from Oceana and the Twenty-Four, trance-channeled by Amritam.

A Special Divine Meditation from Oceana (7/14/2016)

Dear beloveds, this is Oceana. We are bringing you another meditation from the soul world. The soul world wants you all to know that this is a very important time to meditate at night or in the morning, for at least half an hour or longer if you can. We are asking you to meditate and to send light from your heart to your family, friends, and teachers; and if you have a particular saint you are close to, send love and light to them. It is important to meditate at a time when you have no interruptions. Before you meditate, make sure you create the space.

Now I am giving you a meditation: Close your eyes. Say, "Dear Divine, please bless me. Please help me to be more conscious and more loving, and allow me to give to others as well from my heart. Please help me to stay in the state of love, peace, and harmony. I love you, dear God. I love you, dear saints. Please help me to be more conscious and more loving, and help me to open my heart to God, to the saints, and to all the people I love." Then you say, "Thank you, dear ones." And then they give you a beautiful golden ball of light and surround you with it. As you are sitting in the golden light, ask for a blessing. Ask for love. Ask them to give you peace, joy, and happiness and to keep your heart open to loving yourself and others. Then you just sit quietly, and you relax and meditate. You may also repeat, "I love the Divine, I love myself, and I love humanity. Dear Divine, bring peace, joy, happiness, and a deep ability to help others and myself to live lives of service, joy, and healing to myself and others." Then you say, "Dear God, thank you for all your gifts. Please help me to keep my heart open. Thank you, thank you, thank you." Then you sit quietly and surround yourself in golden light. You feel the silence, and you begin to feel joy, peace, and happiness. Then you just sit in the hum until you feel finished, and thank God and the Divine for your life and ask for blessings. This is a new meditation. I will be sending more meditations to you. Please let us know how your meditations are going. With love from Oceana and the Twenty-Four, trance-channeled by Amritam.

Oceana's Special Meditation (2/20/2016)

Dear beloved ones, this is Oceana and the Twenty-Four. Spring is coming, and it is a time of new beginnings, new growth, and new dreams ... when you have new beginnings for abundance, relationships, and new starts ... leaving the past behind. So let go of the past and start new because spring is coming. So this is the time to write down your dreams and hopes for abundance, relationships, and new creations for your life. So our suggestion is to write down your new ideas. Every day, close your eyes and visualize what you want, as if it has already happened, and you will send it out to the universe; you will see it, and then you will let it go. Then it creates itself, and it will come back to you. Be patient. And every day you will visualize in the morning and in the evening, as if it has already happened. It's important to let it go so that it can come back to you. It can be whatever you want ... money, relationships, health, or happiness. Send it out and let it go, and do that every day. With love and blessings from Oceana and the Twenty-Four, trance-channeled by Amritam.

CONCLUSION

Love, peace, harmony, and forgiveness to all from the Divine!

Printed in the United States
by Baker & Taylor Publisher Services

Printed in the United States
by Baker & Taylor Publisher Services